THE NEW STATES OF CENTRAL ASIA AND THEIR NEIGHBOURS

The Council on Foreign Relations publishes authoritative and timely books on international affairs and American foreign policy. Designed for the interested citizen and specialist alike, the Council's rich assortment of studies covers topics ranging from economics to regional conflict to U.S.–Soviet relations. If you would like more information, please write:

Council on Foreign Relations Press
58 East 68th Street
New York, NY 10021
Telephone: (212) 734-0400
FAX: (212) 861-2759

THE NEW STATES OF CENTRAL ASIA AND THEIR NEIGHBOURS

Peter Ferdinand

Editor

PUBLISHED IN NORTH AMERICA FOR

THE ROYAL INSTITUTE OF INTERNATIONAL AFFAIRS

COUNCIL ON FOREIGN RELATIONS PRESS
• NEW YORK •

Chatham House Papers

The Royal Institute of International Affairs, at Chatham House in London, has provided an impartial forum for discussion and debate on current international issues for 70 years. Its resident research fellows, specialized information resources, and range of publications, conferences, and meetings span the fields of international politics, economics, and security. The Institute is independent of government.

Chatham House Papers are short monographs on current policy problems which have been commissioned by the RIIA. In preparing the papers, authors are advised by a study group of experts convened by the RIIA, and publication of a paper indicates that the Institute regards it as an authoritative contribution to the public debate. The Institute does not, however, hold opinions of its own; the views expressed in this publication are the responsibility of the author.

Library of Congress Cataloging-in-Publication Data

The New States of Central Asia and their neighbours / edited by Peter
  Ferdinand.
        p.   cm.
   "Published in North America . . . for the Royal Institute of
International Affairs . "
   Originally published : London : Pinter Publishers, 1994 ; under
the title New Central Asia and its neighbours.
   Includes bibliographical references.
   ISBN 0-87609-173-7
   1. Asia, Central–Foreign relations–1991- 2. Asia, Central–
History.   I. Ferdinand , Peter. II. New Central Asia and its
neighbours.
DK859.5.N48 1994
327.58–dc20
                                                            94-43356
                                                              CIP

94 95 96 97 98   PB   10   9   8   7   6   5   4   3   2   1

CONTENTS

CONTRIBUTORS

Dr Shirin Akiner is Director of the Central Asia Research Forum at the School of Oriental and African Studies in London, Editor of *Central Asia File,* and the author of various publications on Central Asia, including *Islamic Peoples of the Soviet Union* (1986) and (ed.) *Political and Economic Trends in Central Asia* (1993).

Professor Grigory Bondarevsky is a historian, member of the Institute of Sociological Studies of the Russian Academy of Sciences, former Dean of Tashkent University and Vice-Minister of Foreign Affairs of Uzbekistan, as well as an adviser to President Yeltsin. He is a Nehru Award winner, and Chief Editor of the London journal *Ethnic and National Problems.*

Dr Peter Ferdinand is Director of the Centre for Studies in Democratization at the University of Warwick, and was formerly the Head of the Asia-Pacific Programme at the Royal Institute of International Affairs. His book *Communist Regimes in Comparative Perspective* was published in 1991.

Anthony Hyman is currently writing a book on nationalism and independence in Central Asia, and was a Senior Fellow of the Social Science Research Council–MacArthur Foundation (New York) in 1991–3. He is Associate Editor of the journal *Central Asian Survey* (London).

Dr Philip Robins is Head of the Middle East Programme at the Royal Institute of International Affairs. He is the author of *Turkey and the Middle East* (RIIA/Pinter, 1991) and is currently researching a book on Turkish foreign policy.

ACKNOWLEDGMENTS

Original versions of these chapters were presented at study groups at Chatham House. The authors are extremely grateful to the participants for their various helpful suggestions both during and after those meeings.

The gestation of this book has been longer, and the preparation of the final manuscript more hasty, than originally planned. The authors wish to acknowledge the patience and editorial skill of Margaret May and the Publications Department at Chatham House as well as the typing skill under pressure of Clare Kumahor from the Asia-Pacific Programme.

August 1994   P.F.

Central Asia

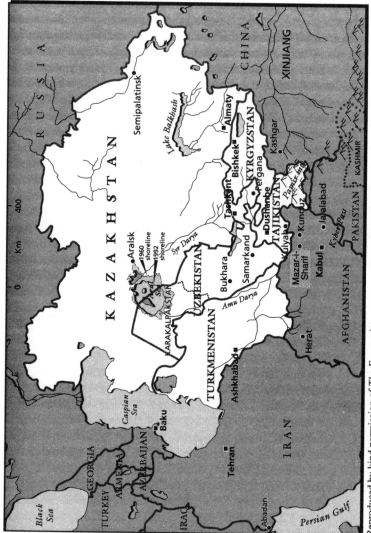

1

INTRODUCTION

Peter Ferdinand

The collapse of communism in Europe and the former Soviet Union (FSU) has transformed world geopolitics. Not only has the balance of power shifted, but the glue holding various political regions of the world together has begun to dissolve. New 'regions' are beginning to emerge, both as political entities and as objects of study.

One of these is former Soviet Central Asia. After a century and more of domination by Russia the republics there have begun to emerge on the world stage in their own right. When in 1992 they effectively had independence thrust upon them, they attracted widespread attention because they had previously been so little known. The purpose of this book is to outline the ways in which they have begun to develop and to interact with their neighbours.

First of all let us outline the region with which we shall be dealing. The epithet 'Central Asia' is not an indigenous term, but was imposed on the region by nineteenth-century Europeans in a vain attempt to establish at least a territorial identity for this protean, tantalizing stretch of land that had for so long survived uneasily in the interstices of great empires.[1] It is indicative of the elusive nature of the region that 'Central Asia' has remained a term without clear definition, used almost at random to refer to the whole or any part of an area that extends from the Kipchak steppes of Central Russia to the Great Wall of China. The reason for this lack of spatial precision is that the question of definition is one that cannot be answered by reference to physical criteria alone, but must take account of – and make a judgment on – such factors as cultural affinities, economic links, historical continuities and political realities, as well as self-perceptions and aspirations. The balance between these different elements is constantly

1

in flux, varying with time and with locality, not necessarily simultaneously: a kaleidoscope of evolving linkages and cleavages, of fragmentation and consolidation.

The Central Asia which will be discussed here is encompassed by the newly independent republics of Kazakhstan, Kyrgyzstan, Tajikistan, Turkmenistan and Uzbekistan. Attempts to categorize the cultural (and therefore likely political) orientation of even this relatively small part of Central Asia tend to founder on the intractable complexities of its historical legacy. Should this region be considered to be part of the Islamic world: an extension, perhaps, of the Middle East? Or does it have more in common with Southeast Asia? Has the experience of over a century of Russian rule given it an indelibly European stamp, or are its neighbours to the east, especially China, likely to exercise a stronger magnetic pull?

Chapter 2 concentrates upon the republics themselves – their origins and history as well as their more recent past. Reflecting the republics' own current preoccupation with this issue, the chapter considers to what extent there ever was a Central Asian identity, and to what extent attempts are now being made in the region to create one.

Chapter 3 examines relations with Russia, in particular whether the two sides can now learn to coexist on equal terms, and the policies of the republics, as well as popular attitudes towards their Russian minorities. The authors investigate the likelihood of military confrontation and the possibilities for economic cooperation.

Relations with the Middle East are considered in Chapter 4. It looks at the rivalry between Iran and Turkey in Central Asia, the attempts of neighbouring Islamic states to spread religious belief in Central Asia, and the economic opportunities, particularly as seen by Israel, Iran and Turkey.

Chapter 5 turns to South Asia. It looks at the responses of India and Pakistan to the emergence of the Central Asian states, and the prospects for economic cooperation. It examines the likelihood of the fighting in Afghanistan spreading further across the frontier, and the impact of the civil war in Tajikistan.

Chapter 6 explores the relationship with China, including an assessment of the effect upon Xinjiang, and upon Beijing's plans for oil exploration and exploitation there; while Chapter 7 briefly summarizes the political, economic and social changes in this emerging region.

As will be clear, not only is the place of Central Asia in world affairs undecided, so too is its character. It, like the world around it, is a region in flux. Its inhabitants are themselves in search of their own identity.

Interaction with their neighbours will be one of the ways in which that identity will be formed. At the crossroads of the Eurasian landmass, Central Asia has the potential either to strengthen or to undermine the stability of its neighbours. Either way this cannot fail to have a significant impact on relations in other parts of the world. The rest of the world, too, can contribute to the course of events there, especially if it is well-informed. It was in the hope of illuminating many of the issues at stake that this book was originally conceived. It goes without saying that the authors of the individual chapters do not have identical views on all the developments in the region, and therefore occasional differences of emphasis and interpretation will occur.

2

POST-SOVIET CENTRAL ASIA: PAST IS PROLOGUE

Shirin Akiner

Where and what is Central Asia?

Geography

The five Central Asian republics together cover a territory of approximately 4 million sq. km (thus close in size to the combined areas of Algeria and Libya), with a combined population of some 55 million. To the north the region is bordered by the Russian Federation, to the east by China, to the south by Iran and Afghanistan, to the west by the Caspian Sea. The distance to an open sea varies between some 2,000 km (to the Black Sea, Persian Gulf and Kara Sea) and over 5,000 km (to the Pacific seaboard). The relief of the region is very varied. It falls into four bands: the steppes of the north, the belt of oases and river valleys of the centre, the deserts further south and the mountains of the eastern and southern periphery. The north is comparatively well endowed with water resources, but in the south there are severe water deficits. There are three main river systems: in the far west that of the Ural and the Emba, which empty into the Caspian Sea; in the centre the head-waters of the Siberian rivers, which flow northwards to the Kara Sea; and in the southeast the glacier-fed mountain rivers that flow westwards to the plains, amongst them the Amu Darya and the Syr Darya. There are a number of inland seas and lakes, the largest being the Caspian Sea in the west, the Aral Sea in the centre and Lake Balkhash in the east. Precipitation is generally low, with the exception of the foothills of the mountains in the southeast. The climate is sharply continental, with an annual range of some 40°–50°C between summer and winter temperatures, and significant variations between south and north: in the southern deserts summer temperatures of 50°C are not uncommon, whereas in the northern steppes 28°C is usually the upper limit. The soil in most parts of Central Asia is fertile, but in the south crop cultivation requires irrigation. The region is rich in natural resources, with very considerable deposits of oil and natural gas, coal, gold, uranium and other valuable commodities.

The northern tier of Central Asia is dominated by *Kazakhstan*. The second largest republic (after the Russian Federation) in the former Soviet Union, it encompasses an area of 2,717,300 sq. km and is thus more than four-and-a-half times larger than Ukraine (601,000 sq. km). The two largest groups are the Kazakhs and the Russians, the former (according to the 1989 census) constituting some 40 per cent (6.5 million) of the total population of some 17 million, the latter approximately 38 per cent (6.2 million). Factors such as the immigration of Kazakhs from other regions (including the return of a few thousand from Mongolia and Iran, descendants of those who fled across the borders in the wake of the Russian revolution and civil war) and the emigration of some Russians from the south, as well as the higher birth-rate amongst the Kazakhs, have served to increase the percentage of Kazakhs in the total population over the past five years, but accurate data are not available. Other ethnic groups of significant size include Germans (960,000 in 1989, but numbers now considerably reduced by the ongoing exodus), Ukrainians (900,000), Tatars (330,000) and Uzbeks (332,000).

The two republics of the plains, Uzbekistan and Turkmenistan, are next in size. Situated in the southwestern corner of Central Asia, *Turkmenistan* (488,100 sq. km) has the smallest population (3.5 million in the 1989 census). Over 70 per cent of the population are Turkmen. There are several other ethnic groups, but most are numerically quite small. The largest are the Russians (334,000), Uzbeks (317,000) and Kazakhs (88,000). The most centrally located of the five republics, *Uzbekistan* (447,400 sq. km) cuts a diagonal swathe across the region from the frontier with Afghanistan in the southeast to the Aral Sea in the northwest. It includes within its boundaries the semi-independent republic of Karakalpakstan (164,900 sq. km). Uzbekistan has a population of over 20 million. This includes 1.1 million in Karakalpakstan. Uzbeks constitute the majority of the population (over 70 per cent), but many other ethnic groups are represented in significant numbers. Russians comprise 1.7 million; other groups include Tajiks (934,000), Kazakhs (808,000, though unofficial estimates put their number at 1 million or above), Tatars (468,000) and Koreans (183,000).

The two smallest republics are those in the mountains of the southeast.

5

Kyrgyzstan (198,500 sq. km) has a population of 4.3 million, of which the Kyrgyz constitute 53.3 per cent. There are also Russians (917,000), Ukrainians (108,000), and Germans (101,000); however, many from these groups are now leaving Kyrgyzstan. In the south, in the Osh province, there is a fairly compact group of Uzbeks (in all, some 550,000 in the republic). *Tajikistan* (143,100 sq. km), which includes within its boundaries Badakhshan (63,700 sq km), formerly an autonomous region, now semi-independent, has a population of approximately 5.1 million (1989 census), of which 62 per cent are Tajiks. These include some 160,000 so-called 'Mountain Tajiks', or Pamiris, in Badakshan, who are only distantly related to the Tajiks 'proper'; the Pamiris are almost all Ismaili Muslims, unlike other Tajiks, who are Sunni. The remainder of the population included, in 1989, 1.2 million Uzbeks (24 per cent of the total) and 388,500 Russians (8 per cent of the total). An unknown number of these have now fled the republic; the Slav population has probably been reduced by at least a third. The Uzbeks live in compact settlements, mostly in the northwest; they do not appear to have left in significant numbers.

The historical legacy
The single most remarkable feature of Central Asian history has been the manner in which the region has continually both attracted and generated movements of population. Some of these have been the result of imperial conquest, others (in the more distant past) a consequence of sudden irruptions of nomad hordes. Trade, pilgrimage and the quest for knowledge (not to mention sheer curiosity) have also prompted large and small groups of people to traverse the region, as part of an ongoing interchange of philosophies, religions, technologies, commodities, languages, scripts, foodstuffs, items of clothing, 'high' culture, popular culture and much else besides. Thus from the very earliest times, Central Asia has been a centre for cross-cultural fertilization. Indeed, some have argued that syncretism is its hallmark. Others see it as a cultural continuum so dynamic that it has been able to absorb external influences without any loss of individuality. Evidence can be found to support either view, but what is certain is that Central Asia, with all its diversity, has shown an extraordinary ability continually to recreate itself, to accept change and yet to maintain continuity.

The history of the region prior to the twentieth century falls into two broad divisions: that of the nomads and that of the settled peoples. The domain of the former was in the north (modern Kazakhstan and

Kyrgyzstan) and the far south (southern Turkmenistan); that of the latter, the fertile oasis belt that stretches from the borders of western China to the shores of the Caspian Sea, running diagonally across the southern half of the region. The first urban settlements in the south appeared around 1500 BC, probably founded by peoples of Iranian origin. From the sixth to the fourth centuries BC this region was under the control of the Persian Achaemenian empire; politically this was of little more than nominal significance, but the cultural impact was strong, as is evidenced by the fact that Zoroastrianism was widely practised. At the end of the fourth century BC Alexander the Great overthrew the Achaemenians and he and his successors introduced a new element, that of Hellenism, to southern Central Asia. Subsequently, from the middle of the third century BC, the eastern part (present-day Uzbekistan) formed part of the Graeco-Bactrian state, while the western part (present-day Turkmenistan) was incorporated into the Parthian empire, and thus became subject to different cultural influences. However, the entire region was linked by the so-called 'Silk Roads', the transcontinental trade routes that for almost two millennia serviced an economic network encompassing China, India, the Middle East and the Black Sea basin.

In the third century AD, Iran, now ruled by the Sassanids, re-established its hegemony over southern Central Asia. It was to remain the major political, cultural and economic force in the region for many centuries. However, it was itself transformed by the Arab invasions of the seventh century, which, in Islam, brought not only a new belief system but also a new social order and a new epistemology. Iran embraced this new world and subsequently became the physical as well as the intellectual conduit whereby it was introduced to Central Asia. The Arabs used Khorasan (northern Iran) as a springboard for their conquest of Khwarezm (approximately equivalent to the territory of modern Karakalpakstan), Transoxiana (north of the Amu Darya) and Fergana. The ancient cities of Merv, Bukhara and Samarkand were drawn into the cultural orbit of the Caliphate and within a century had become important centres of Muslim learning. In time, they produced some of the finest scholars and the greatest buildings in the Islamic world. The purely Arab presence was soon withdrawn, however, and administratively the region remained under the jurisdiction of Khorasan, thus still very much within the Iranian sphere of influence. The first independent Muslim state in Central Asia, that of the Samanids, was founded in 875 by an Iranian dynasty from Khorasan, which, having established a power base in Bukhara, built up an empire that, at its height, exercised suzerainty over

Transoxiana, Khwarezm and large tracts of Iran and Afghanistan.

The early history of the northern half of Central Asia (Kazakhstan and Kyrgyzstan) is obscure. Archaeological excavations have revealed traces of a highly developed artistic tradition, but little is known of the peoples involved. However, the annals of neighbouring sedentary peoples, especially the Chinese, throw some light on the chronological sequence of events. It is principally from these sources that we learn of the eastward surge of the powerful Ephthalites (White Huns), who dominated much of Central Asia during the fourth to the sixth centuries AD. They were eventually displaced by another nomadic wave, that of the Turks. The first record of the presence of the latter in Central Asia dates from the mid-sixth century. The Turks rapidly gained control of a vast territory, including part of the route of the 'Silk Roads'. Their empire survived in one form or another, despite frequent threats from the Chinese, until the mid-eighth century, when they were overthrown by yet another wave of Turkic invaders, the Uighurs. The progression of Turkic incursions into the region continued up until the early sixteenth century. However, by the tenth century, the earlier inhabitants had been either expelled or overwhelmed, to the extent that much of Central Asia came to be known as 'Turkestan' ('land of the Turks'), a term which is still sometimes used today.[1] The implication was not that the region was united under a single ruler, which was certainly not the case, but that the majority of the population spoke Turkic languages. Some of the Turkic tribes remained nomadic, but others, in the south, adopted a sedentary way of life. There they converted to Islam; the first Turkic Muslim state was that of the Karakhanids (c. 932–c. 1165), who established themselves in Bukhara (after overthrowing the Samanids), but extended their rule further to the east, to the Ili and Tarim rivers (modern Xinjiang). The sedentarized Turks in the cities of Transoxiana were heavily influenced by Iranian culture, and in the Bukhara-Samarkand region Farsi continued to be the main vehicle for administration, literature and trade, despite the emergence of Turkic literary languages (e.g. Karakhanid and later Chaghatai).[2]

The last major nomad invasion of Central Asia was that of the Mongols in the early thirteenth century. Their first appearance in the region was accompanied by havoc and destruction; later, however, they melded with the local population and adopted their language and culture. Tamerlane, the fourteenth-century potentate (1336–1405) who subdued Transoxiana, Transcaucasia, Khorasan and a large part of northern India, exemplified the fusion of these different elements. An Islamicized, Turkified Mongol, he made Samarkand his capital and beautified it with superb buildings and gardens, encouraged science and the arts, yet retained the restless ferocity, even barbarity, of a nomad chief. After his death, his empire (which included most of the southern belt of Central Asia, but not the north) gradually disintegrated into ever smaller units, ruled over by local warlords. By the sixteenth century, two centres had emerged as the chief regional powers, the Khanates of Bukhara and Khiva. The former and larger (which adopted the designation of 'Emirate' in the eighteenth century) occupied a territory that coincided approximately with that of modern Uzbekistan, but also included parts of Turkmenistan, Tajikistan and Afghanistan. Khiva, somewhat smaller in size, was situated to the south of the Aral Sea and occupied areas of Turkmen, Kazakh and Karakalpak lands. In the early eighteenth century a third power base took shape, that of the Khanate of Kokand, whose territory lay to the northeast and encompassed parts of modern Kyrgyzstan, Tajikistan and Uzbekistan (including Tashkent). These states, together with their smaller dependencies, were engaged almost ceaselessly in murderous, tortuous territorial disputes.[3]

The northern steppes were dominated by the nomadic Kazakhs who, by the sixteenth century, had coalesced into three 'Hordes' (known in Kazakh as *zhus*, 'part'), which were, in effect, tribal confederations. Each had its own territory (summer and winter pastures) and a hierarchical structure of command under the rule of a hereditary leader (the Khan). The lands of the Little Horde lay to the north of the Caspian Sea, of the Middle Horde in the centre (between the Tobol and Irtysh rivers) and of the Great Horde in the southeast, extending into Xinjiang. The Hordes were united for brief periods, but, as with the Khanates in the south, they were frequently engaged in internecine hostilities. At the same time, they, and the neighbouring Kyrgyz tribes to the east, were under constant pressure from the Oirots (Jungarians), nomads from the northeast. The latter were defeated by the Manchus in 1758, and some of the Kyrgyz and Kazakhs were incorporated into the Chinese empire (Chinese claims on Kazakh territory until recently included a swathe of territory extending as far west as Lake Balkhash and Almaty). At this time Islam had barely begun to penetrate these regions. It gradually gained a stronger foothold during the nineteenth century, but in the steppes and mountains of the northeast it was never practised with the same degree of orthodoxy as amongst the settled peoples of the oasis belt.

The Russians had had diplomatic contacts with Central Asia from the mid-sixteenth century. By this time the development of maritime links between Europe and Asia had caused the balance of trade to shift from land to sea routes. The trade that remained was mostly of a regional nature. However, routes to the west, towards Muscovy, were, from a geographical point of view, relatively free of obstacles. In time this relationship came to be of major economic significance. Yet there were also dangers for Central Asia in this easy access. In the course of the eighteenth century the Russians began to extend their power south of the Urals; the Kazakh Hordes came ever more firmly under Russian domination, until, in the first half of the nineteenth century, the power of their Khans was finally broken. In the second half of the century Russian troops moved southwards, to capture Tashkent in 1865, Samarkand in 1868; the Emirate of Bukhara became a Russian Protectorate that same year, followed by Khiva in 1873. In 1876 the Khanate of Kokand was fully annexed, losing all semblance of autonomy.

The Tsarist administration, once in place, met with less resistance than most other colonial regimes. Economic links between the 'centre' and the Central Asian periphery were strengthened, underpinned by the construction of a railway network that also served security and defence needs. There was little interference with native institutions, but some of the local elites were influenced by Russian ideas. Moreover, they were exposed to a major influx of Muslims from other parts of the Russian empire (principally Crimean and Volga Tatars, and Azerbaijanis), who introduced some reformist trends in education (the so-called *jadid* movement). However, political awareness, in the Western sense, remained very low, and on the eve of the First World War the changes in Central Asian society were still slight and mostly superficial.[4]

The Soviet era

Soviet rule was established in Central Asia between 1918 and 1922. This was the prelude to a period of fundamental social transformation. The first step in this direction was the creation, within the framework of the Soviet Union, of proto-nation-states. This territorial division, known as the National Delimitation of Central Asia, was based on the assumption that ethnic and linguistic affiliations coincided, and that together they formed the markers of 'national' identity. In Central Asia, however, although awareness of 'national' group identities was by no means entirely absent (the accounts of nineteenth-century ethnographers, philologists, historians and travellers use ethnic designations for the various peoples, indicating that such distinctions were indeed recognized), they were not nearly as important as clan or tribal affiliations. The new territorial divisions, which cut across the boundaries of the Khanates and the tribal groupings, were an attempt to obliterate previous forms of self-definition by providing an alternative focus for regional, sub-state identities (the state identity being Soviet). Within its own terms of reference the Delimitation was successful, since without any exchange of peoples, some 85–95 per cent of the total population of the main ethnic groups were encompassed within the borders of their own titular republics. The one group that suffered severe territorial loss was the Tajiks: the largest Persian-speaking group of the region, they had lived for centuries as one people with the sedentarized Uzbeks.[5] It was impossible to make an equitable territorial division between these two groups. The Uzbeks, being more numerous and more powerful, secured by far the larger share of the disputed lands, including the historic Persian-speaking centres of Bukhara and Samarkand. The Tajiks have never ceased to resent this and it remains a cause of serious friction.

The National Delimitation took place in 1924. It embraced all the territory that had been under Tsarist rule and further incorporated the Protectorates of Bukhara and Khiva (which had had a brief period of semi-independence as People's Soviet Republics between 1920 and 1924). Uzbekistan and Turkmenistan were immediately given full Union Republic status, while Tajikistan, including the 'Pamir Province', later renamed Gorno-Badakhshan, was created as an Autonomous Republic within Uzbekistan. Kazakhstan and Kyrgyzstan were given the status of Autonomous Republics (the latter was initially an Autonomous Province) within the Russian Federation. In 1929 Tajikistan acquired Union Republic status, followed by Kazakhstan and Kyrgyzstan in 1936; Karakalpakstan, originally part of the Kazakh Republic, became an Autonomous Republic within the Russian Federation in 1932, and was transferred (with the same status) to the jurisdiction of Uzbekistan in 1936; today, as noted, it has semi-independent status. There was some readjustment of borders during the Soviet period (e.g. Khojent province was transferred from Uzbekistan to Tajikistan in 1929), but in broad outline the territories of the newly independent republics of post-Soviet Central Asia are those that were delimited in 1924.

The physical creation of the Soviet Central Asian republics was followed by a comprehensive campaign to modernize and Sovietize the region. This involved major feats of social engineering. The key mobilizing factors were collectivization and mass education.

Collectivization was carried out in the early 1930s by workers, predominantly Russian, who were sent from other parts of the USSR to industrialize Soviet farming. The President of the USSR, Kalinin, re-marked in 1929 that the aim of Soviet policy was 'to teach the people of the Kyrgyz steppe, the small Uzbek cotton grower and the Turkmenian gardener the ideals of the Leningrad worker'.[6]

Mass education served not only to create a more efficient work force, but also to politicize the population and thereby incorporate it into the new system. According to the first Soviet census (1926), the average rate of literacy amongst the Uzbeks, Tajiks and Turkmen was less than 3 per cent, and amongst the Kazakhs and Kyrgyz 6 per cent. A massive programme of teaching, training and the provision of textbooks was initiated, and by 1932 it was estimated that some 50 per cent of the population had achieved a basic level of literacy. This had risen to almost 70 per cent by 1939 and in the 1970 census was recorded as over 99 per cent.[7] Compulsory education for all children, male and female, was introduced, beginning with a limited primary curriculum which was gradually increased to an eight-year, later a ten-year, and finally an eleven-year programme of study.

The educational process was saturated with ideology. Other aspects of the modernization campaign were likewise, though sometimes less obvi-ously, motivated by ideological concerns. The creation of official 'national' languages, literatures and histories, for example, far from being a purely academic exercise, was part of the struggle to remould the intellectual responses of society. The primary goals were, on the one hand, to inculcate a sense of 'national' identity, but on the other, to ensure that this remained subordinate to an overarching Soviet identity. The new literary languages were based on selected local dialects, but their vocabu-laries were expanded (mainly by a heavy influx of Russian and interna-tional terms) in ways that enabled them to convey the material and ideological concepts relevant to Soviet society. The message was further reinforced by the forms of graphic representation: in the 1920s, use of the Arabic script was still permitted, but it was replaced by the Latin script around 1930 and by the Cyrillic in 1940. The new national literatures drew on local realia, but by using Soviet or Western genres in prose and poetry, they also contributed to the development of different perceptions, different terms of reference.[8] The national histories, which traced the emergence of each ethnic group from its 'ethnogenesis' through to its incorporation into the Soviet polity, were likewise aimed at giving substance and legitimacy to the new system.[9]

Alongside the efforts to instil new norms and values, a concerted onslaught was unleashed against every visible vestige of pre-Soviet culture. The chief target was, inevitably, Islam. Until the end of the 1920s it was treated with uneasy tolerance, but thereafter, with minor variations in tactics, the official attitude for the next 50 years was one of implacable hostility. The social and organizational infrastructure of Islam was destroyed by such measures as the abolition of religious schools, colleges, charitable endowments (*waqf*), law courts and tithes. The great majority of mosques were closed and most of the religious leaders either silenced (by death, long imprisonment or flight abroad) or co-opted into the service of the new regime. Such factors as the emancipation of women (whereby they acquired equal legal status with men, were encouraged to work outside the home and to abandon all symbols of male oppression, including the veil) and the abolition of the Arabic script, though not directly connected with religion, were nevertheless part of the campaign to undermine Islam and to destroy traditional society. The process of social transformation was hastened by the purges of the 1930s, which not only eradicated all potential sources of opposition, but also created such an all-pervasive climate of fear that it resulted in self-censorship, which in turn produced what can only be termed defensive amnesia.[10] Almost the only feature of pre-Soviet society to survive this pressure was the network of family and clan relationships. Virtually invisible to the outsider, such relationships provided a degree of protection against the arbitrary excesses of the system. This element of continuity in the most intimate areas of life provided a counterbalance to the enormous changes that were taking place in the public domain. It acted as a safety valve, enabling a high degree of social transformation to be effected, while yet preserving an inner equilibrium.

The social and cultural transformation of Central Asia was accompanied by political and economic integration into the Soviet system. A semblance of independence was provided by the creation of national emblems and institutions (flags, anthems, constitutions, embryonic governments, branches of the CPSU, of the Leninist Young Communist League, of trade union organizations etc.). In reality, however, all such bodies were entirely subordinate to the central government and/or all-Union parent organizations; like the symbols, they were of little more than cosmetic significance. Areas such as defence, foreign policy and macroeconomic planning fell entirely within Moscow's jurisdiction. Investment allocation was decided in accordance with all-Union priorities, not those of an individual republic. In Central Asia, this led to extremely lop-sided economic development, with much emphasis on the production of primary commodities, but little attention devoted to the creation of

13

manufacturing industries. In turn this produced a high level of dependence on interrepublican trade. The main sectors of the Central Asian republics' economies were agriculture, the extractive industries (mainly oil, gas, coal and minerals) and energy. There was some heavy engineering (especially in Uzbekistan), some metallurgy (including the processing of aluminium and uranium in Tajikistan) and several large petrochemical plants. There were also a number of military-industrial complexes, including the nuclear testing site at Semipalatinsk and the Baikonur space centre (both in Kazakhstan) and testing sites for chemical and biological weapons (in Uzbekistan and possibly elsewhere). Most of the larger enterprises, and all the military complexes, were under the direct control of Moscow. The republican governments not only had no control over them, but were not given access to production figures.[11]

In the second half of the 1980s the first signs of a 'national awakening' began to surface in the Central Asian republics, prompted in large measure by anger at the manner in which Central Asia was treated as the scapegoat for the corruption that was endemic in the Soviet system. Resentment at Moscow's high-handed treatment of the local ruling elites was palpable throughout society (and in Kazakhstan in December 1986 spilled over into open protest). There were at this time, too, the faint beginnings of an Islamic revival in some areas of Uzbekistan and Tajikistan; the first sociopolitical movements also began to appear, mostly prompted by local environmental and cultural concerns. Declarations of sovereignty were made by all the Central Asian republics in 1990, but as with similar declarations made by other Soviet republics, the intention at this time was certainly not to leave the Union; rather, the declarations signalled a desire for greater autonomy in running their own internal affairs.[12] In the all-Union referendum of March 1991 the Central Asians voted overwhelmingly to maintain the Union.[13] The immediate response of many (including senior officials) to the abortive coup of August 1991 was to support the action of the coup leaders. When the coup failed, first Uzbekistan, then Kyrgyzstan, Tajikistan and Turkmenistan proclaimed their independence. However, no formal steps to secede from the Union were initiated and it was generally supposed by the public (who had nowhere been consulted and who were taken by surprise by these announcements) that they would remain a mere formality, with no substance.

On 8 December 1991, however, the presidents of the three Slav republics – Russia, Ukraine and Belarus – announced, without prior consultation with other heads of Soviet republics, that they were forming their own, three-member Union. There was no mention of the fate of the Soviet Union but without these three republics it was clear that it could not survive. Thus, by default, without a liberation struggle or change of leadership, the Central Asian republics suddenly found themselves independent. The framework within which they had been created and had existed for over 70 years was no more. A fortnight later a summit meeting was convened in Almaty, and as a result of deliberations held there, a protocol on the formation of the Commonwealth of Independent States (CIS) was signed by the leaders of eleven of the Union republics, including all five Central Asian republics which inisted on being accepted as 'co-founders' of the CIS, not merely subsequent signatories. They were admitted to the United Nations in March 1992 and have since joined numerous other international and regional organizations. All the Central Asian leaders have emphasized their intention to avoid being drawn into any exclusive ethnic or ideological grouping. Each republic has established direct diplomatic and commercial links with over a hundred countries in the Middle East, the Far East, Southeast Asia, Europe, America and Africa.[14] Domestically, measures have been undertaken in every sphere to consolidate political and economic independence.[15] Some steps have also been initiated to facilitate intraregional cooperation. Substantial progress has been made in most areas, although much more still remains to be done before *de jure* independence becomes a practical reality.

Political organization

Traditional power structures

Traditional (i.e. pre-Tsarist) Central Asian society was divided into tribes. These were largely, though not exclusively, based on genealogical lines. Within the tribes there was a complex system of hierarchically structured subdivisions. In some areas, for example amongst the Turkmen, there were five or six levels of subdivision (sub-tribes, sub-sub-tribes, clans, sub-clans etc.). The basic unit was the nuclear family. This could be extended along blood lines (or by marriage) to form larger groupings, which could in turn be combined to create broader networks. At every level, within every unit, there was a clear, patriarchal leadership structure. Within the family, it comprised the father and senior male members; within a clan or larger grouping, it would be centred on a (male) figure of authority who, by his lineage, wealth and talent, was

15

able to command the respect and unquestioning allegiance of his peers. Similarly, such a leader would give his loyalty (and consequently that of his whole clan) to the leader of a larger grouping at the next level of seniority. Thus, society was held together by vertical chains of loyalty which reached upwards, layer by layer, to the supreme leader of the group, the tribal Khan. There was some flexibility in the system, since it was possible, in theory at least, to shift allegiance from one leader to another. The strength of the genealogical ties, however, and the cohesive force of the pyramidal structure of society made this a rare occurrence.

During the Soviet period, these traditional structures became the basis for what was, in effect, a parallel system of power. The internal linkages were almost imperceptible to the uninitiated: such factors as name, place of birth or physical appearance provided few clues as to clan or tribal affiliation. During the years of Soviet rule, behind a façade of ideological commitment, the regional groupings continued their long-standing power struggles, but now using the system itself as a weapon. Today it is gradually being acknowledged that indigenous elites used the purges of the 1930s as means of eliminating their rivals. Even when the physical annihilation of rival groups was no longer their aim, members of a given clan would strive to position themselves in such a way as to hold a monopoly on power in 'their region', which in turn was a cell in a much larger network, encompassing at its largest extent the entire republic. It was thus, through skilful manoeuvring and manipulation of the system, that within a few decades of the imposition of Soviet rule, in each of the republics one of the traditional groupings had established itself as the dominant local force, a position which most of them still hold today.[16] In Tajikistan, for example, the clan based on Leninabad/Khojent dominated the political life of the republic from the 1930s – and resentment over this was the chief factor in the civil war which broke out in 1992.

During the Soviet period the close-knit nature of the clan was maintained and even enhanced, but membership of such a group was gradually broadened to include not only those who were related by blood, but also those who had shared a common experience, such as school, college, or professional training. Eventually, too, a distinctly criminal element began to emerge. This may have been present earlier, but if so, it was not obvious to outsiders. Since the 1980s the clan system has increasingly been referred to as 'the mafia' and it is rumoured that some groups have now established links with criminal circles abroad. Whether or not this is true, it remains only part of the story: clan loyalties are still, for the majority, a source of mutual help and protection in the conduct of their normal affairs. Such bonds have many advantages, especially in times of hardship. However, they are undoubtedly a hindrance to the establishment of Western-style multi-party democracy: first, because it is largely personal allegiances, not issues, that continue to dominate people's thinking; and, second, because political leaders are themselves bound to reward fellow clan members for their support as soon as it is within their means to do so. In trade and industry too preferment, more often than not, is given on the basis of traditional ties rather than merit.

Formal political structures
Kazakhstan, Kyrgyzstan, Uzbekistan and Turkmenistan have presidential systems of government, with separate executive, legislative and judicial bodies. Tajikistan has a similar system, but in 1992 it temporarily abandoned the post of president; in early 1994 it seemed probable that it would soon be restored.[17] In all five republics there are three levels of administration: the national government; the provincial governments (at *oblast'* level); the regional governments (at *rayon* or district level). The main functions and organs of state are replicated at each of the two lower levels and in theory each of these levels exercises a considerable degree of autonomy. In practice, however, there are two chains of subordination: one to the administrative level immediately above, the other directly to the president of the republic. The provincial governors are nominated by the president, and the regional administrative heads by the provincial governors; thus there is a strong element of personal loyalty leading upwards through the system. This is a potential source of conflict, since it creates parallel power structures, with no clear demarcation of authority and jurisdiction. This is reflected in the lack of clarity between the functions of the legislative and the executive bodies at the subordinate levels: the latter are becoming increasingly more independent, circumventing the checks and balances that originally existed, and acting as additional organs of presidential authority.

Since the collapse of the Soviet Union there has been some degree of constitutional reform in all the republics. However, the trend has been to give the presidential incumbent ever greater powers. The nature of presidential rule in Turkmenistan is more blatantly dictatorial than in, for example, Kyrgyzstan, a republic that has a reputation for being more democratic. The constitutional positions in the two states, however, are far from dissimilar. The same is true elsewhere in Central Asia. Personality cults, reminiscent of the Brezhnev period as well as that of the medieval Khans, have emerged in some places. The presidential hold on power has been further strengthened in all the republics by the creation of government-sponsored political parties. These have unrivalled (and in some cases unique) access to the media, as well as many other administrative privileges. They serve as mouthpieces for official views, and at the same time act as a symbolic counterbalance to independent political parties. They include a high proportion of 'establishment' figures, many of whom are senior former communists.[18]

Independent political parties

The political culture of Central Asia is very different from that of the West. The real issues are, as discussed above, power and patronage – first on a personal basis and, second, on a clan or regional basis. The few individuals who are genuinely interested in initiating political debate (most of whom are professionals who have studied in Moscow or elsewhere in European republics of the former Soviet Union) have attracted very little popular support. Not only is the nature of the discourse alien to the region, but the very idea of criticizing and openly challenging established authority is deeply distasteful.

The first attempt at creating an opposition party was the formation of *Birlik* ('Unity') in Uzbekistan in late 1988. An 'informal' (in the Soviet sense) social movement, Birlik was principally concerned with issues relating to the national culture (primarily the official status of the Uzbek language) and the environment (primarily the desiccation of the Aral Sea). Initially, it was greeted with some enthusiasm; not only were the questions it raised of concern to a large proportion of the population, but the very novelty of unofficial mass meetings generated its own excitement. However, this was not enough to sustain public interest. Moreover, the government quickly adopted the movement's main arguments and, in so doing, gained additional respect for what was generally perceived to be a wise and flexible approach. Uzbek was given the status of state language and some concessions were made on environmental issues. Birlik was thus marginalized almost at its inception. Personality clashes within the movement prompted the formation of a splinter group *Erk* ('Freedom' or 'Free Will') within little more than a year. At first the authorities were inclined to favour Erk: it was granted official registration (and thus became a fully-fledged 'party' with various legal rights, as opposed to an 'informal' movement, which had no official status) and seemed in danger of becoming a puppet opposition. However, the government soon lost patience with Erk and by 1993 this group was being subjected to almost as much harassment as Birlik. Both parties were subsequently banned; the leading activists went into hiding, eventually to seek refuge in Moscow or countries outside the CIS.

Independent sociopolitical movements began to appear in the other Central Asian republics at almost the same time as in Uzbekistan, but for the most part were even less successful in gaining popular support. In Kazakhstan, the Nevada-Semipalatinsk anti-nuclear movement, founded by the poet Olzhas Suleimenov, had clear goals and was better organized than most; in August 1991, in the immediate aftermath of the abortive coup to unseat President Gorbachev, the movement achieved its main goal, an end to nuclear tests at the Semipalatinsk site. Thereafter, efforts to give the movement a broader political base met with suspicion and distrust; allegations of financial improprieties multiplied and by the end of 1993 what remained of it had been irrevocably discredited. Independent political activity thereafter acquired an overtly nationalist bias. The main Kazakh party is at present *Azat* ('Freedom'), which is small in actual numbers, but very vocal in its demands for a greater 'Kazakhification' of society. *Alash* (a reference to Kazakh history), an even smaller party, combines Kazakh nationalism with Islamic revivalist sentiments. Amongst the Russian population, analogous groups are also beginning to appear. The best organized at present is *Lad* ('Concord').[19] Cultural centres and organizations provide a focus for tentatively nationalist sentiments among the smaller ethnic minorities, such as the Uighurs, Tatars and Germans. In all these cases the chief issue is the protection (and, if possible, enhancement) of ethnic rights.

In Kyrgyzstan, the first sociopolitical movement to make an impact on public opinion was *Ashar* ('Mutual Help'); its chief aim was to help the unemployed, homeless, rural youth who, from 1990 onwards, began to move to the outskirts of Bishkek, sometimes setting up picket lines to draw attention to their plight. Parties with a more specific political orientation soon appeared, but the turnover of membership and leadership is so rapid that it is difficult to discern any continuity of aims. Currently the most active groups are *Erkin Kyrgyzstan* ('Free Kyrgyzstan'), which has put forward its own draft for a new state constitution, and the Democratic Movement of Kyrgyzstan; together they form an active opposition to the government. The Communist Party, recently re-registered, also provides substantial opposition; it is by far the most popular party and may well regain power in the not too distant future. There are also strong nationalist tendencies in Kyrgyzstan, and these are represented by *Asaba* and *Ata Meken*.[20]

In Turkmenistan no opposition of any sort is permitted. The informal movement *Agzybirlik* ('Unity') seemed to attract support in 1990, but now is little more than a small, loose association of like-minded individuals. The main centres for Turkmen opposition to government rule are outside the republic, mainly in Moscow.[21]

In Tajikistan, now that the situation has deteriorated into civil war, conditions are so fluid and so complex that terms such as 'opposition', 'rebel' and 'democrat' have very little meaning. Individuals, including leaders of factions, frequently change their orientation; alliances are formed and broken depending on the prevailing circumstances. The movement *Rastokhez* ('Rebirth'), originally a mildly democratic organization, has undergone so many transformations and splits that it survives in little more than name. The Islamic Revival Party attracted some support for a while and after its official registration in 1992 seemed likely to play a role in government; after the outbreak of prolonged armed conflict, however, the movement was banned and its leaders went into hiding or fled to Afghanistan or Iran. Its constituency appears to be mainly in rural areas, with little urban support.

Islam and 'state ideologies'

Before the establishment of Soviet power the Muslims from a nomadic tradition (Kazakhs, Kyrgyz and Turkmen) were far less orthodox in their beliefs and practices than were those from the sedentarized communities (Uzbeks and Tajiks). The Soviet experience had a homogenizing effect: it reduced all to a state of equal ignorance about religious matters. At the same time, however, Islam became, for both groups, a form of cultural defence. For the great majority of Central Asians, it represented a symbolic link with the world of their forefathers. It found expression in the token observance of Islamic ritual in ceremonies connected with rites of passage (e.g. births, deaths, weddings). The ritual may not have been correctly performed, it may not have been understood, and it may not even have been Islamic (all traditional practices were assumed to be Islamic), but the perception was that it was 'right', that it imparted dignity and legitimacy to the proceedings. The chief markers of Islamic identity during this period were male circumcision, which was maintained almost without exception, and dietary precepts, although these were gradually eroded, especially in urban areas. The role of 'parallel' Sufi movements in keeping Islamic belief alive was greatly exaggerated by foreign (and later Soviet) commentators. Knowledge of basic religious teachings was almost entirely eradicated.[22]

During the mid-1980s, there were attempts to revive more orthodox Islamic practices. The so-called 'Wahhabis', small groups of individuals (in all, numbering probably no more than 10,000), mostly located in the Fergana Valley, on the borders of Uzbekistan, Tajikistan and Kyrgyzstan, spontaneously and without external sponsorship began to seek out knowledge about Islam and to live according to its tenets. They did not have a wide following, but they aroused some interest, especially among urban intellectuals, who were beginning to chafe under Moscow's tutelage. Perhaps the most significant contribution of the 'Wahhabis' at this time was that they rekindled a general awareness of the moral and intellectual qualities of Islam.

Towards the end of the 1980s, perestroika and glasnost finally began to have an effect in Central Asia. The chief consequence of this was a more accommodating attitude towards Islam. This volte-face was greeted with surprise, but also great enthusiasm, by the indigenous population. Several new mosques were opened and informal religious classes were set up in many areas. The ruling elites, although still officially members of the Communist Party and therefore forbidden to take part in religious ceremonies, nevertheless began to give official encouragement to the Islamic revival. This was in large part a political gesture, an astute move to establish new credentials for themselves, rooted in local culture and not, therefore, dependent on Moscow. After the collapse of the Soviet Union, this stood them in good stead. Islam provided a ready replacement for Soviet ideology. It was not, however, to be allowed to develop freely: from the very beginning, the respective governments exerted firm control over religious practice. The religious functionaries were expected to conform to official policies; those who did not were persecuted much as they would have been during the Soviet period. Fear of fundamentalism was used as an excuse to muzzle any form of opposition in Uzbekistan; the situation was not much better in the other republics. This state-sponsored form of Islam was in fact welcomed by many Central Asians, especially by the more educated, Westernized urban dwellers who were happy to see Islam accorded a more prominent place in the cultural and ceremonial spheres of life, but did not want it to play a normative role in everyday affairs. In rural areas, especially in the Fergana Valley, a more extremist form of Islam is reputed to be taking hold. The Islamic Revival Party has its main base here. However, since it has been banned in all the republics (after the brief period of official recognition in Tajikistan in 1992), it is impossible to be sure of the extent of its support.

Alongside Islam, the national culture in all its various manifestations is being promoted. This is part of a conscious effort to create new 'state ideologies', new frameworks of individual and communal identification to give emotional content to independence. The tools that are being employed in this new phase of nation-building are very similar to those that were used during the Soviet period, when the aim was to provide legitimization for the new republics and the national identities. Linguistic questions are again receiving much attention. There is a conscious (though not consistent) effort to replace Russian or international words with Arabic, Persian or Turkic equivalents (for example, *darulfunun* instead of *universitet*). There has also been much discussion of the question of scripts: whether or not to retain the Cyrillic, and, if it is to be abandoned, whether to adopt the Latin or the Arabic script in its place. Two years ago public opinion was much in favour of the latter and many adults and children are still eager to learn it, since it represents a link with the pre-Soviet past. However, in political circles there is general agreement that the adoption of the Arabic script would send misleading signals to the West, implying an Islamic, and hence fundamentalist orientation; this, it is believed, would hinder chances of securing Western aid. There has accordingly been a campaign in favour of a move to the Latin script.[23] All the republics except Tajikistan have now taken preliminary decisions to phase in the Latin script over the next few years. Given the vast expense involved, not to mention the enormous social and cultural disruption, it is by no means certain that they will in fact do so.

There are also calls for the rewriting of history, to correct the biased version provided by Soviet textbooks. However, there is as yet no agreement as to how, or by whom, this revision is to be undertaken. Undoubtedly, there is a pressing need for a fundamental review of the interpretation of Central Asian history that was presented by Soviet scholars, but there is a real danger that, as before, there will be little attempt to employ objective criteria: the past will again be used to justify the present, merely from a different perspective. Selected aspects of the past are already being emphasized (as during the Soviet period) in order to project a particular image of society, and also to stress underlying continuities and hence to legitimize the current regimes. In Uzbekistan, for example, Tamerlane has been elevated to the status of founding father of the nation. A clear parallel is drawn between this exemplar of the all-powerful ruler and President Islam Karimov, the present-day father of the nation. In Kazakhstan and Kyrgyzstan, cultural role-models (folk musicians, poets and writers), as well as leaders who brought unity to the divided tribes, are being commemorated. In Turkmenistan, the legacy of ancient Parthia is being stressed, perhaps to counterbalance the Islamic contribution; in Tajikistan, there is a revival of interest in Zoroastrianism – likewise an attempt to show the diversity of the cultural heritage.

The 'Silk Roads' has become a potent image throughout the region. It serves as a reminder that Central Asia was once an important link in the economy of the known world, and holds out the promise that it might become so again. Cultural and historical bonds with specific countries are given prominent coverage whenever there is an exchange of high-ranking delegations. Thus much has been written and broadcast, especially in the Soviet period, about the shared heritage of, for example, South Asia and Uzbekistan (there are indeed close cultural links, and Indian films have long enjoyed phenomenal popularity in the region – see Chapter 5). Ancient links with Turkey and Iran are likewise frequently aired. The history of Central Asia is so rich and varied that there are genuine grounds for these and many other such claims. They are a useful adjunct to diplomacy, but should not be taken as indications of political orientation. A casual perusal of the Central Asian press is sufficient to reveal that a similar 'historical justification' is found for any desirable contact. Pragmatism was and is the guiding principle of Central Asian politics. Economic self-interest may well dictate a strengthening of links between, for example, China and Kazakhstan, or Turkmenistan and Iran, but it is more than likely that the respective Central Asian governments will continue to balance such a relationship with other contacts.

The economy

The nature of the economies of the Central Asian republics (primarily oriented towards the production of raw materials) made these republics more dependent than others on All-Union structures. Consequently, the sudden disintegration of the Union caused greater dislocation in Central Asia than elsewhere. Moreover, the infrastructure of government and administration in these republics was weaker: in January 1992, there were few trained professionals who were able to assume full operational responsibility for the wide range of tasks that confronted the newly independent governments. It was not that there were no competent Central Asian statisticians, economists, lawyers, bankers etc., but rather that the previous experience of such people had been limited to fulfilling particular functions within a much larger system. Knowledge of Western systems (or even languages) was very restricted. In addition to these problems, the Central Asian republics were almost wholly dependent on Moscow for communication and transport routes. Thus, even after these republics had acquired formal independence, they remained bound by innumerable links to the 'centre'. Social factors also contributed to the region's economic difficulties. The standard of living was appreciably lower than elsewhere in the Soviet Union; moreover, the rate of demographic increase was much higher, and the proportion of potential wage-earners to dependents per family unit was smaller. By the end of the Soviet period this was already placing severe strains on the state's ability to provide adequate employment and social services for the population. After the collapse of the Union, budgetary subsidies from the central government ceased and the republican governments were left to shoulder the ever-increasing costs of social welfare.[24]

Given these conditions it was vital, but also extremely difficult, to implement economic reform. Prices were liberalized in January 1992, in line with the measures adopted in Russia, but some control was retained over basic commodities (outbreaks of civil disorder greeted the price rises in Uzbekistan and Turkmenistan, and extreme discontent was voiced elsewhere). Privatization programmes had already been initiated in Kazakhstan in 1991, and there had been similar moves in Kyrgyzstan. It soon became clear, however, that the governments in both these republics had seriously underestimated the difficulties involved in this process. None of the essential structures in such key areas as law, banking, accountancy, insurance, surveying and valuing, taxation and independent supply networks were in place.

There were also specific local factors that exerted a negative influence. In Kazakhstan, for example, the native Kazakhs had neither the disposable wealth nor the cultural predilection to acquire property. They alleged that the 'foreigners' (Russians, Germans, Uzbeks, Jews, etc.) did not suffer from these constraints and eagerly availed themselves of the new opportunities. The result was a serious increase in inter-ethnic tensions as Kazakhs came to feel that they were being robbed of their ancestral lands. Asset-stripping of enterprises due to be privatized, and the extortion of bribes from prospective clients, were common practices. By the summer of 1993 there was widespread dissatisfaction with the process. Senior Kazakh officials publicly acknowledged that mistakes had been made and that many of the privatizations that had already been completed would have to be cancelled because of legal irregularities.[25] It was also admitted that communal enterprises functioned less well after they had been transferred to private ownership; the rate of bankruptcies amongst newly privatized small businesses was recently estimated to be 95 per cent.[26]

In Kyrgyzstan, official statements on the privatization process conveyed a relatively positive impression, but the reality was that here, too, there were very considerable problems.[27] In the three other republics, privatization is proceeding at a much slower pace and, on the surface at least, appears to be slightly more orderly. In Uzbekistan, some of the dwellings set aside for privatization have been transferred to their occupants free of charge. It was intended that in 1994 the programme would be accelerated and include the privatization of land. But then, for reasons that will be outlined in Chapter 3, President Karimov suddenly announced an acceleration of the programme in January 1994.

The five Central Asian republics had initially intended to remain within the rouble zone. However, encouraged by US government and IMF/World Bank support, Kyrgyzstan elected to launch its own national currency, the som, on 10 May 1993. The immediate consequences were disastrous. There was an acute shortage of the new banknotes, but at the same time fines were introduced for trading in roubles. Many private shops were forced to close, while banking operations in Bishkek came to a virtual standstill. President Karimov of Uzbekistan and President Nursultan Nazarbayev of Kazakhstan, who had not been consulted in advance – a breach of previously agreed procedures – were incensed by the Kyrgyz action. The border with Uzbekistan was closed (causing major food shortages in neighbouring Osh) and gas supplies were halted until the Kyrgyz President, Askar Akayev, had made his personal apologies to the Uzbek President.

By June 1993 it was clear that Turkmenistan was also intending to launch its own currency. Uzbekistan and Kazakhstan, however, were determined to remain with the rouble, even after the Russian Central Bank's announcement of 23 July decreeing the withdrawal of pre-1993 rouble notes. Both republics signed the multilateral agreement with Russia 'On the creation of a new-type rouble zone' on 7 September, and there was a further Kazakh–Russian agreement on 23 September, 'On unification of the financial systems of Russia and Kazakhstan'. However, Russia subsequently demanded financial guarantees (billions of dollars, according to President Nazarbayev) which were felt to be unacceptable. Consequently, despite the fact that Kazakhstan's foreign currency and gold reserves were far from sufficient to support its own currency at a viable rate, the republic decided to introduce the tenge on 15 November. Uzbekistan launched a transitional coupon currency (the sum-coupon) at almost the same time. Meanwhile, Turkmenistan had already introduced its national currency, the manat, on 1 November. By the end of 1993 Tajikistan was the only Central Asian republic still within the rouble zone. The Tajiks agreed to introduce full implementation of all the parameters of the Russian finance and credit system within six months, and in return, the Russian Central Bank undertook to supply the Tajik government with a credit of 120 billion new (1993) roubles, to be paid in instalments. By early 1994, however, little progress in fiscal and monetary reform had been made by the Tajik authorities and large quantities of the new roubles were already leaking into the neighbouring republics, where the Russian currency continued to enjoy greater prestige than the new national units. Further consignments of roubles from the Russian Central Bank have been suspended for the present.

Throughout the region, prices for industrial and domestic commodities have been rising month by month. Salary and social welfare benefits are increased at regular intervals, but are unable to keep pace with inflation. Academic and other 'non-essential' institutions are frequently unable to pay employees' salaries. Many industrial plants have been forced to close because of a lack of essential supplies; this is often part of a vicious circle of debt in which enterprises cannot pay for the supplies because they themselves are owed huge sums of money by their clients. There has been a considerable fall in industrial and agricultural output in all the republics.[28] Unemployment is soaring (in Kyrgyzstan, by mid-1993, at least a third of the workforce was unemployed). The state governments are unable to provide adequate compensation, thus poverty levels are also rising. In Kyrgyzstan, for example, official estimates set the cost of a basket of basic consumer items at 200 som per month, while average salaries are 100 som; the minimum level for wages and pensions has recently been set at 45 som. Not surprisingly, it is now estimated that 90 per cent of the Kyrgyz population live below the poverty line.

It is clear that the Central Asian republics are currently in a state of severe economic decline. However, if they can stave off total collapse, the longer-term outlook is more hopeful. All the republics are well endowed with resources; they also possess young, reasonably numerate and literate populations, and political systems that, because of their rigid authoritarianism, are often easier to do business with than those elsewhere in the former Soviet Union.[29] This combination of factors is beginning to attract serious direct investment from abroad. The oil and gas industries in Kazakhstan have so far been the major beneficiaries. The largest deal to date (estimated to be worth $20 billion, spread over 40 years) was signed between Chevron Overseas and Kazakh Tengiznefte-gaz. In mid-1992, Elf Aquitaine secured rights to develop a 19,300 sq. km area southwest of Aktyube (formerly Aktyubinsk); the first well had been drilled by December 1993 and although production is still some way in the future, the indications are that the operation will be successful. In December 1993, the Kazakhstankaspishelf State Company signed a preliminary agreement with a consortium of seven leading Western oil companies (BP, British Gas, Mobil, Shell, Statoil, Total and Agip) to carry out a feasibility and environmental study of the offshore oil and gas deposits in the Kazakh section (100,000 sq. km) of the Caspian Sea. British Gas and Agip are also negotiating with the Kazakh authorities for the rights to develop the rich Karachaganak oil and gas/condensates field in northwest Kazakhstan. The most pressing problem to be resolved is that of the pipelines: at present they feed into the Russian grid and it is therefore Moscow that has the final say on export quotas. The favoured route at present is to the south, but whether overland or under the Caspian Sea has yet to be decided. It will, however, take several years before new pipelines are in place and Russia's role will thus continue to be of crucial significance for some time to come.

Other resources that are attracting foreign attention are gold and, to a lesser extent, uranium. Uzbekistan has several major deposits of gold and, with a current output of some 85 tonnes per annum, is the seventh largest producer in the world. An investment package of $103 million has been agreed with a Western consortium, headed by the Canadian-based transnational Newmont, to refine tailings from the open-cast mines in the Bukhara-Navoi district. There has also been Canadian interest in the gold deposits of Kyrgyzstan, although here the negotiations have been marred by allegations of serious financial misconduct on the part of senior Kyrgyz officials. The Prime Minister, Tursunbek Chynygshev, was forced to resign over this issue in December 1993. Tajikistan also has sizeable deposits of gold, but, apart from the political instability in the country, these are located in areas that are not easily accessible; thus they are not likely to be commercially viable in the near future.

Social, transport and environmental issues

Demography

At the beginning of the twentieth century the population of the region was approximately 10 million; thus there has been an increase of over fivefold to its current 55 million, largely owing to high birth-rates amongst the indigenous peoples, especially in rural areas, and falling death-rates.[30] As in other parts of the developing world, some 50 per cent of the population are under 20 years of age. However, ongoing immigration into the region has also contributed to the rapid increase in population. There were three main waves: in the 1920s and 1930s, when development pro-grammes in the economic and social spheres were being energetically pursued by the central government; during the Second World War, when many industries and scientific institutions were relocated from the vulner-able western Soviet republics to Central Asia, and also 'unreliable' peoples were deported there *en masse* (e.g. Crimean Tatars, Volga Germans, Black Sea Greeks); and in the 1950s and 1960s, when there was a new burst of economic activity, especially in connection with the development of the 'Virgin Lands' of Kazakhstan. As a result of these different influxes, all the Central Asian republics are today multiethnic, although the ratio of immigrants to the indigenous population varies considerably between the different republics. There is now some outmigration of ethnic minorities in progress; this will help to relieve pressure on the region's resources (although undoubtedly causing other problems, especially in industry). There is also a slight fall in urban birth-rates, but in rural areas they remain very high and will certainly place increasing strain on social services, accommodation and employment. There are concerns that in the rela-tively near future the carrying capacity of the region will be stretched to such a point that it will not be able to provide the basic necessities of life, and that major social tensions will be the inevitable outcome.

Urbanization

In all the republics the level of urbanization rose during the Soviet period, although at a rate somewhat below that of the average for the Soviet Union as a whole. The republic with the largest urban population is Kazakhstan (58 per cent); Tajikistan has the lowest (33 per cent). Much of the increase in the urban populations can be ascribed to the influx of immigrants from other parts of the Union. The indigenous Central Asian peoples showed very low mobility and for the most part remained in the areas in which they had traditional family ties. Over the past few years this has begun to change. The economic crisis has brought unemployment and poverty to rural areas and this has forced members of the younger generation to move to the cities in search of work. However, the urban drift is still sporadic and relatively circumscribed; there are as yet no shanty towns on the edges of Central Asian cities. Traditionally, the highest levels of population density were in the well-watered valleys of the south; this is still true today, but industrialization and the expansion of large-scale agriculture have helped to colonize the northern belt and to encroach on the margins of the deserts. The central and southern regions are still very sparsely populated.[31]

Health and education
Health and education indicators in the Central Asian republics were raised to levels far higher than in other developing countries, although lower than in developed countries (including the western republics of the USSR). Average infant mortality rates in the first year of life per 1,000 live births range between 29.0 in Kazakhstan and 58.2 in Turkmenistan; in rural areas the figures are somewhat higher. Life expectancy at birth for males ranges between 64 and 66 years, for females between 68 and 73 years (Kazakhstan being at the higher end of the scale, Turkmenistan at the lower).[32] Primary and secondary education are free and compulsory; there are a variety of facilities for tertiary education in each republic (selection is by examination). The national Academies of Sciences include specialist research institutes, some of which enjoy an international reputation (e.g. the Institute of the Desert in Turkmenistan). It is unlikely that the newly independent republics will have the financial resources to maintain the health and education provision at current standards. Serious lapses are already beginning to occur.

Communications
Communications and transport networks within the five republics are serviceable, but greatly in need of modernization. Formerly the best links were with Moscow, and those that formed part of all-Union networks. Intraregional and intrarepublican connections were weak. Post-independence, the motorways and railways are still functioning, although standards of maintenance are noticeably lower. Air links between Moscow and the Central Asian republics used to be cheap, regular and frequent. Domestic and intraregional flights, however, were often eccentrically scheduled and frequently relied on the services of small, outdated aircraft.

Telephone links within the region were likewise extremely poor. Some of these services are now being upgraded. Telecommunications are receiving priority treatment and the capital cities now have reasonably good telephone exchanges. Facsimile machines are also becoming more readily available. International communications are therefore somewhat easier than they were before independence, although within the republics intercity facilities are still little more than rudimentary. Fuel shortages, a consequence of the disruption of interrepublican economic relations since the collapse of the Soviet Union, have caused a severe cutback in domestic air travel (Bishkek airport, for example, was closed for most of 1993 owing to inadequate supplies of petrol), but international links are being expanded. Companies such as Lufthansa, Turkish Airways, Iran Air, Pakistan International Airlines, Air India, Uzbekistan Airways and Kazakhstan Airways provide regular services to Europe, the Middle East, the Far East and South Asia. Charter flights are also much in demand. This expansion is all the more remarkable since, prior to January 1992, there were almost no direct international flights to and from Central Asia. There are now plans in hand to upgrade Tashkent airport and possibly also the airport at Almaty.

The environment

The over-intensive developmental policies pursued by the central government created severe environmental problems in all the Central Asian republics. Unbearable strains were placed on the fragile ecological balance of the region, which led to various forms of dysfunction. Water management has caused the greatest problems: the soil in most places of southern Central Asia (southern Kazakhstan and the other four republics) is potentially productive, but requires irrigation. In the past, water resources were carefully husbanded. During the Soviet period, however, grandiose schemes were introduced, with the aim of 'making the desert bloom'. Nowhere in the world have large-scale irrigation regimes been problem-free and Central Asia is no exception. So much water was drawn off from the rivers that in several cases the flow was reduced to dangerously low levels. The most notable examples are the two rivers which used to feed the Aral Sea, the Amu Darya and Syr Darya. The latter now peters out some distance from the Sea, while the former reaches it only in wet years. Deprived of this vital inflow, the Aral Sea has been shrinking at a catastrophic rate. Over the past 30 years the surface level has dropped by 13 metres and its area has been reduced by over one-third (it currently covers less than 44,000 sq. km). The effects of this desiccation include a small but significant climate change; the loss of several species of flora and fauna, leading to an impoverishment of the region's biodiversity; and the devastation of industries such as fishing, canning and musk-rat farming which, until the 1980s, were the mainstay of the local economy. International aid is now being sought to stabilize the condition of the Sea (which has already split into two and shows signs of further fragmentation). Many other problems have arisen as a result of the ill-conceived and badly constructed irrigation systems. These include the rise in groundwater level, owing to the lack of adequate drainage and the seepage from unlined canals, also the secondary salination and alkalization of the soil through leaching. The construction of shallow, flatland reservoirs has exacerbated the situation by encouraging evaporation and thus further depleting the region's limited water resources. Lack of an effective monitoring system has encouraged negligence and waste.[33]

Other environmental problems in Central Asia have received less public attention, but several of them are as serious as those connected with water management. Land erosion in Kazakhstan, a consequence of the 'Virgin Lands' policy of the Khrushchev era, is reaching extremely severe levels in some areas. It is also a major problem in Tajikistan and Kyrgyzstan, where the intensification of sheep-rearing has led to over-grazing and the compacting of the soil, owing to the formation of myriads of tracks; this has denuded the thin layer of topsoil, making it highly vulnerable to wind action. Deforestation has accelerated this process.

The comparatively low level of industrial development has meant that industrial pollution is not as serious a problem as in other parts of the former Soviet Union. However, with few exceptions, the technology used in the mining and processing industries is old, inefficient and environmentally harmful. Thus, though the affected areas are fewer in number, in the immediate vicinity of an industrial plant there is almost invariably severe ecological damage. Conditions at the aluminium works in Tursunzade (Tajikistan) and in petrochemical plants such as that in Navoi (Uzbekistan) are particularly bad. Uranium and gold-mining operations produce toxic waste that is not adequately protected. Military-industrial complexes have given rise to a specific range of problems. The worst-affected region is undoubtedly that of Semipalatinsk (Kazakhstan), the nuclear test site, where prolonged exposure to radiation has caused severe abnormalities in humans and animals and will have an incalculable effect on the health and well-being of future generations; the soil and water have also been contaminated, thus affecting the food chain. In Uzbekistan, there are known to be testing sites for chemical and biological weapons (for example, on the island of Vozrozhdeniye in the Aral Sea), but little is known of the effects on the environment.[34]

Prospects for regional stability

The prospects for regional stability in Central Asia in the near future are good. In four of the republics there is strong, centralized, authoritarian rule. In the fifth, Tajikistan, the chaos of civil war persists. The chief concerns of the population in all five republics are those connected with physical survival – the struggles to obtain food, fuel and accommodation. No opposition leaders have yet emerged who are able to offer credible solutions to the present problems, and the great majority of Central Asians are prepared to continue to place their trust in the current ruling elites. In Turkmenistan and Kyrgyzstan, the mandate of the incumbent presidents was reconfirmed by almost unanimous support in nationwide referendums held respectively on 15 and 30 January 1994. Presidents Karimov and Nazarbayev are not due for re-election for some years, but both have indicated that they expect to remain in office for the foreseeable future. In the parliamentary elections held in Kazakhstan in March 1994 the President's party gained majority support.[35] In Tajikistan, as noted, the post of president was suspended in 1992, after the overthrow of President Rahman Nabiev, but the current acting Head of State, Emomali Rakhmonov, has made it clear that he supports a revival of the presidency and that he would not be averse to holding this post himself.

Relations between the five republics are complicated by rivalries and long-standing suspicions (often with their roots in pre-Tsarist times), as, for example, in the relationship between the Kazakhs and the Uzbeks. During the Soviet period, priority was given to developing links with Moscow, not with the neighbouring republics. However, since 1992 some progress has been made towards regional cooperation. In January 1993, the five Central Asian Heads of State agreed on a symbolic change of terminology to signal the intention to work towards greater unity: the Soviet designation *Srednyaya Aziya* ('Middle Asia'), which included only the four southern republics, was replaced by *Tsentral'naya Aziya* ('Central Asia'), a term that in Russian had formerly been reserved for territory further to the east but now is used specifically to refer to the five former Soviet republics considered here. President Nazarbayev subsequently emphasized that this did not herald the creation of a specific Central Asian confederation, but that it did pave the way for closer economic rapprochement. In early 1994, more concrete proposals for the integration of the Uzbek, Kazakh and Kyrgyz economies were announced. There is some collaboration in matters concerning law and order, and defence. Efforts to coordinate policies to alleviate environmental degradation are also in hand, particularly as regards the Aral Sea.[36] If these good intentions are to be given substance, however, it is essential that the necessary institutions and formal mechanisms for cooperation be created. There has as yet been little progress in this direction.

The longer-term prospects for stability in Central Asia are less en-couraging. First, there is the real possibility of internal fragmentation, brought about by clan or regional hostilities. The civil war in Tajikistan is a warning of what might occur. Here, an element of ideological conflict between so-called Islamicists, neo-Communists and democrats undoubted-ly exists; but in essence, it is a power struggle between the two largest clan groupings, those of the north (Khojent) and those of the south (Kulyab), with smaller groups (e.g. those of Garm, Hissar, Badakhshan) casting their weight on the side of whichever of the two offers the most favourable conditions. Coalitions are made and broken at a bewildering rate, as the balance of power constantly shifts from one group to another. The conflict has been further complicated (and may well be prolonged indefinitely in the border regions) by 'clientism', as external forces lend their support to one or other faction. The situation elsewhere is, by comparison, stable; however, there are similar tensions in all the repub-lics which could, under pressure, rapidly deteriorate into violent clashes, if not the actual dismemberment of the state. In Uzbekistan there is tension between the traditional power bases of Samarkand, Tashkent and Fergana. In Kyrgyzstan there is acute disaffection amongst the southern group of clans, who openly resent the dominant role played by the northern group (President Akayev and many of the leading members of the government are from this group). The main tribal confederation in Turkmenistan is that of the Ahal-Tekke; it is unlikely that there will be a serious challenge to its hold on power, although there are rumours of friction with members of other tribes, such as the Ersary and Yomut, whose position is now strengthened by easier contacts with fellow tribes-men in Iran and Afghanistan. The situation in Kazakhstan, however, is the most finely balanced. Here there are not only clan rivalries (between the three Hordes), but also tensions between the two largest ethnic groups, the Kazakhs and the Russians. The latter live in compact groups in the north and at present have sufficient power in the areas in which they constitute the majority not to feel unduly threatened by the growing 'Kazakhification' of the republic. However, should there come a time when they feel discriminated against, or dissatisfied with the safeguards provided by the central government, they would undoubtedly seek secession, either to establish an independent state of their own or to unite with Russia. They would certainly have Russia's support in this and there would be little that the Kazakhs could do to prevent such a move.

A second potential threat to the stability of the region is mass social unrest. Unemployment, inflation and the general breakdown of social

33

services have brought real hardship to the population at large. This, added to the humiliation and anger caused by the collapse of the Soviet Union, and disillusionment with the fruits of independence, has already caused widespread alienation amongst the young, especially in rural areas, where conditions are far worse than in the cities. Cleavages are deepening between the generations, between the countryside and the urban centres, and most of all between various social sectors, in particular between the 'haves' and the 'have-nots'. The danger of a 'social explosion' if material conditions do not improve in the near future is widely acknowledged. It is not impossible that this would take the form of an extremist, xenophobic Islamic movement. This might be encouraged by external sponsors (a combination of Saudi money and Iranian idealism could prove to be a highly inflammable mix), but the roots are already there, within the region itself: false 'foreign ideologies' (democracy just as much as Marxism–Leninism) are held to be responsible for society's ills, and Islam is seen by many, even those who do not actively practise it, as something pure and true. There is a distinct, though as yet small movement in this direction amongst university-educated young Central Asians who, like their blue-collar compatriots, are disillusioned by their experiences of Western values.

A third threat comes from the criminalization of society. Corruption has reached astronomic proportions. Crimes of violence are also on the increase. The law enforcement agencies are undermanned, underpaid and demoralized, hence they offer little protection, and inspire even less confidence. Drug-trafficking has now been added to the other problems. The cultivation, use and illegal trading of narcotics has increased exponentially over the past few years. It has battened on to the traditional clan networks, forming a powerful criminal underworld. It is generally accepted that links have been established with foreign 'mafia' groups, not only in the CIS, but also in Western Europe, Southeast Asia, the Middle East and Latin America.[37] There are fears that arms and nuclear-related materials either already form part of these smuggling operations or soon will do so. The tactical weapons that were stationed on Kazakh territory have now all been withdrawn to Russia; the nuclear warheads still stationed there are under Slav control and appear to be well-guarded (President Nazarbayev has finally agreed that they, too, should be withdrawn).[38] However, the danger exists that terrorist organizations, or aspiring nuclear states, might nevertheless succeed in acquiring some of this strategic arsenal. Given the deteriorating economic and social conditions, it is not improbable that some Central Asians will be tempted to assist in such operations.

A fourth form of instability is represented by the minority groups. There has been no organized discrimination against them, but there is a general perception that 'ethnocracies' are being created, in which those who do not belong to the titular nationality will be treated as second-class citizens. The language laws, which require that all official business be conducted in the state language, are felt to be symptomatic of a move to exclude the minorities from public life. This has prompted those who can find employment and accommodation elsewhere (inevitably, these are mainly the most highly qualified) to leave Central Asia. There has been a wave of emigrations from all the republics, but especially from Tajikistan (prompted by the civil war) and Kyrgyzstan. This exodus of skilled workers and professionals is a serious blow to the already fragile economies of these newly independent states.[39] The republican governments would like to stem the haemorrhage, but are hampered by nationalistic considerations.

The issue of citizenship has brought the question into sharp focus: some of the minority groups (most notably the Russians) insist that only dual citizenship will provide them with the security and reassurance that they feel is lacking at present. The governments of Kazakhstan and Uzbekistan find this unacceptable, insisting that the minorities must choose where their loyalties lie. In Turkmenistan, however, where there are far fewer minority groups, the President has agreed to allow dual citizenship. In Kyrgyzstan, the question is still being fiercely debated: President Akayev does not wish to alienate the large Slav and German populations by refusing outright to accept the concept of dual citizenship, but the Kyrgyz nationalists are fiercely opposed to the idea and he cannot afford to ignore them.[40] Until the minority groups are fully incorporated into society politically, economically and culturally, these tensions will remain and will constitute a threat to stability.

Central Asia, not for the first time in its long history, is in flux. The forces for and against stability are evenly balanced. If the economic situation begins to improve and confidence returns, it is likely that the republics will consolidate their independence and achieve a high level of prosperity. If, however, the tensions within society are heightened, the region could descend into internecine civil strife, as in Tajikistan. The situation is complicated by the fact that it is not merely domestic events but also the influence of external forces that will determine the outcome. These relationships will be examined in the following chapters.

3
RUSSIAN FOREIGN POLICY AND CENTRAL ASIA

Grigory Bondarevsky and Peter Ferdinand

Relations with Moscow before 1991

Throughout the years of the Soviet Union, from 1920, Central Asia was as dependent upon Moscow as was any other region in the country. Being poor, but possessing abundant natural resources which could be exploited with capital, it needed enormous investment from outside. Given the ban on foreign direct investment, however, only Moscow could provide this. Turkmenistan was already benefiting towards the end of the 1920s from large investments from the centre to increase cotton production and so reduce the Soviet state's need for imports from Egypt. But with the funds also came ambitions to transform the traditional way of life. The Bolshevik leadership sought to pacify and to Sovietize the local peoples. In practice that also implied Russification. This came through the collectivization of agriculture at the end of the 1920s, when workers from industrial parts of Russia were sent to Central Asia, and elsewhere, to industrialize Soviet farming. It should be noted that collectivization in Central Asia did provoke an ethnic and religious response. The Fergana Valley in Uzbekistan, a centre of Islamic orthodoxy, saw a renewal of the civil war conflict between anti-Soviet basmachi guerrillas and the Red Army. As during the civil war, the basmachi were again ruthlessly suppressed. 'By 1941, of the 25–30,000 mosques open in 1920, only about 1000 remained. Moreover, all of the 14,500 Islamic religious schools were forcibly shut down, and fewer than 2000 of the approximately 47,000 clerics survived. By the outbreak of the Second World War, the traditional Muslim religious establishment in Central Asia and the Caucasus had been destroyed.'[1]

After the Second World War Moscow continued to attempt to transform the Central Asian economy, although without the same social transformation. It did not, however, bring lasting and self-sustaining success. First there was the whirlwind of Khrushchev's Virgin Lands scheme, which opened up vast tracts of Kazakhstan, imposed Ukrainian methods of farming upon land for which they were ill-suited, and transferred large numbers of outsiders, primarily Slavs, into the region to work on this scheme. Then followed large-scale investment for enormous irrigation schemes in Uzbekistan and elsewhere to develop cotton production so as to supply textile factories in Russia. Even more land was turned over to intensive cotton production. Initially this too brought increased yields. Yet by 1980–82 growth in per capita income appears to have come to a complete halt.[2] And, as mentioned in Chapter 2, the insatiable demand for water began to deplete even the largest rivers such as the Amu Darya and the Syr Darya, whilst the Aral Sea contracted alarmingly as river-water dried up. These changes produced an ecological disaster, with land becoming increasingly salinated and people suffering serious disease from environmental pollution.

Despite all the infusion of roubles, the last decades of the Soviet Union were marked by an increasing concern in Moscow about the relationship between the five republics of Central Asia and the rest of the Union. These republics continued to endure the lowest standard of living, their industrial workers had the lowest productivity, and they had the highest birth-rate and the poorest ability to speak Russian. The last two facts were a source of growing concern for the Soviet army high command, since an increasing proportion of conscripts for military service would in future years have to come from Central Asia, given the declining birth-rate in other parts of the country. Central Asia seemed the least positively integrated region in the Union as a whole, and this would have serious implications for Soviet defence.

Moreover, since the plans for the future development of the agriculture of the region were predicated upon the diversion of water from rivers in Siberia, the interests of the Central Asian republics clashed with those of other parts of the Union. This conflict of interests seemed set to grow, as environmentalists in Russia condemned these plans because of the irreparable damage they might do to the Siberian environment. At that time there was no institutional mechanism whereby the republics of Central Asia could consult with one another on issues of common public policy, so they could not have pressed a common policy position even if they had worked one out. At the same time the republics remained heavily dependent upon Moscow for substantial resources to support local industries. Furthermore, the chief transport links between Central Asia and the rest of the world all stretched northwards through the rest of the USSR. Although, for example, the railway linking Kazakhstan with Xinjiang in China had been virtually completed, the actual stretch crossing the frontier (a few kilometres) remained unlaid, the victim of the confrontation between the USSR and China since the early 1960s.

Despite all these grounds for concern, until the advent of perestroika the leadership in Moscow followed a policy of benign neglect towards Central Asia as far as political control was concerned. The ruling and Russified local elites accepted that their relationship with Moscow was akin to that between a younger and an elder brother. Sometimes they expressed this in effusive terms. In return local leaders were allowed to rule the republics as they pleased. It subsequently became clear that at least some of them practised corruption on a massive scale. As noted in Chapter 2, clan and tribal ties played a vital part in the structure of political control, despite the official communist ideology.

Party officials appointed from Moscow to leading positions apparently either failed to alert the centre to the corruption and enormous over-reporting of economic success, or were ignored. The most spectacular manifestation of this concerned the massive irrigation schemes which were reportedly established in the 1970s. Achievements were hugely exaggerated, yet Moscow took action only when, allegedly, a new Soviet spy satellite was ordered by ground controllers to turn its cameras on the irrigation schemes in Central Asia as a way of calibrating its instruments, and the supposedly well-established dimensions of these schemes were shown to be grossly distorted.

All of this was typical of the era of stagnation of the later Brezhnev years throughout the USSR. It was perestroika that launched efforts from Moscow to try to remedy the situation. Ironically, it was also perestroika that aroused the first signs of positive protest against Moscow, a trend which became more marked as time went on. The catalyst was the replacement of the First Secretary of the Communist Party of Kazakhstan and member of the Politburo of the whole party, Kunaev, in 1986. Gorbachev, newly elected Party General Secretary in Moscow, decided to introduce tighter control. He appointed a Russian, Gennady Kolbin, as the new First Secretary. He also began to talk determinedly about the need to stamp out corruption wherever it was found. He was actually trying to use Kazakhstan as a example for the introduction of greater discipline throughout the USSR. He was not attempting specifically to make any change in policies towards minorities. In Alma-Ata, however, Gorbachev's moves were perceived as an attempt to reformulate the unwritten understanding with Moscow, under which local leaders would be allowed a free reign provided they did not try to achieve independence. The disorders were quelled only after three days of rioting on the streets of Alma-Ata. Kolbin tried to be an energetic defender of the interests of Kazakhstan. Yet these events opened a new era of uncertainty in relations between Moscow and Central Asia. Could the old-style leadership in the region cope with the new-style leadership emanating from Moscow?

In practice Gorbachev had greater preoccupations than this, and so he refrained from imposing his new ideas too strongly on minority areas. In any case, despite his railing against corruption in these areas, he actually behaved as though he believed that the nationalities question in the USSR had basically been solved. Indeed he encouraged decentralization as a way of taming the excessive power of the party and state authorities in Moscow, and he did so without any apparent apprehension that this might lead to the break-up of the USSR. He, like his predecessors, seemed to accept that the victory of socialism and the approach of the communist ideal had engendered a friendship among all the peoples of the USSR, which had led to the formation of a new historical and social entity called 'the Soviet people'.

Unfortunately conflicts did break out in a number of areas, in some cases with serious loss of life: Alma-Ata, Sumgait, Nagorno-Karabakh, Andizhan, Tbilisi, Osh, Baku. Moscow belatedly realized that it was necessary to remodel the Soviet polity and to dismantle the imperial system for managing the economy, culture and social relations. This put on the agenda a radical amendment of the 1977 Soviet constitution and the drafting of a new Union treaty to replace the 1922 treaty which had marked the founding of the USSR. However, the drafting process in the commissions and committees of the USSR Supreme Soviet was very slow and was furthermore sabotaged by the party machinery. This led Gorbachev to adopt a different tack. Direct negotiations began between the leaders of the Union republics at Novo-Ogarevo near Moscow in 1991.

As a result of prolonged and quite heated debates an agreement was reached on a stage-by-stage signing of the new treaty. This was to be signed first by the leaders of the Russian Federation, Kazakhstan and Uzbekistan. In September and October 1991 the leaders of another six republics were to put their signatures to the treaty. By then the Baltic states had already left the Soviet Union.

The abortive coup between 19 and 21 August radicalized the situation and released new political processes. It put paid to the rule of the CPSU and launched democratic movements. But in the Central Asian republics, where the influence of the party apparatus was still very strong, the leaders of the coup were not condemned straight away, even though they had demanded the restoration of imperialist centralism.

Nevertheless the leaders of the Union republics, including those in Central Asia, refused to sign the new Union treaty, despite the fact that there were greater possibilities for implementing it now that the centralizing rule of the Communist Party had ended. The initial reaction of the Russian leadership was quite severe. President Yeltsin announced that Russia's pledge to renounce all territorial claims against other republics applied only to the members of the future confederation. This was taken as a serious threat, especially to Ukraine and Kazakhstan. In the latter a potential target for Russian claims was the mineral-rich region of eastern Kazakhstan, where the predominant nationality is Russian. Naturally this aroused indignation, in Kiev as well as in Alma-Ata. After lengthy negotiations and mutual recriminations, the Russian leadership decided to abandon its territorial claims, at least for the time being.

The effect of the establishment of the CIS in December 1991 (see Chapter 2) upon the leaders in Central Asia was earth-shattering. It is fair to say that right up to that moment not one of the leaders of the republics of Central Asia had counted on the disintegration of Soviet territory, still less anticipated that it would take place so suddenly. This was despite the fact that since August there had been incessant and complex dialogues, meetings, disagreements, and contacts between all the capitals of these republics, as well as with Moscow and Kiev. In a sense, therefore, the Central Asian republics had independence thrust upon them. The leaders had not worked to bring it about and indeed they were inclined to prefer the basic features of the old system, since it supported their rule and allowed for the transfer of resources into the region from other parts of the USSR via Moscow.

Relations between the Russian Federation and Central Asia, 1991–3.
It is fair to say that immediately after the attempted coup in August 1991, Russia's relations with the newly independent states of Central Asia were far from being the highest priority of the new Russian administration. The task of enlarging and staffing a new Russian Foreign Ministry, as opposed to a Soviet one, was both vital and daunting. President Yeltsin

was concerned with transforming the Russian economy into a genuine market, and he knew that he would need financial assistance from the West to cushion the Russian people against what he hoped would be short-term hardships. In addition he was grateful for all the moral support which leaders of Western countries had displayed for him during the struggle against the plotters. As a result Russian foreign policy became strongly pro-Western.

Indicative of these priorities is the fact that Foreign Minister Kozyrev first visited Central Asia in April 1992, by which time US Secretary of State James Baker had already been there three times on official visits. Russian embassies in the region were established only after those of Turkey, Iran, China and the United States.

In addition the Russian leadership assumed that Central Asian dependence upon Russia would persist for a whole host of reasons: their own country's industrial might; the dependence of the Central Asian republics upon innumerable economic links with Russia; the preponderance of Russian engineers and technicians in the Central Asian economies, and of Russian administrators in government service; the various social and ethnic contradictions within and between the republics, the lack of their own armed forces and the stationing there of units from the Turkestan and Central Asian military regions; and, finally, the fact that the republics lacked their own foreign policy apparatus.

The Central Asian republics were therefore obliged to throw themselves into diplomatic activity so as to make other countries take notice of them, Russia included. They succeeded beyond anyone's expectations, and possibly even their own. The fact that they became members of the UN was in itself no surprise, since this flowed directly from the governmental agreements establishing the CIS at Novo-Ogarevo in December 1991. Nevertheless membership was achieved more quickly and more easily than anyone anticipated. This was in no small measure due to the skilful diplomacy of the presidents of these republics, especially those of Uzbekistan and Kazakhstan, who turned to their advantage the sometimes contradictory interests of the Muslim states of the Middle East, the United States and China.

What came as more of a surprise was the scale of the diplomatic links which they managed to set up in a short space of time. For example, Kazakhstan established diplomatic relations with over 40 states in seven months. Uzbekistan was almost as successful. Four republics became full members of the Economic Cooperation Organization (ECO) in February 1992, whilst the fifth, Kazakhstan, became a temporary associate member.

This organization had originally comprised only Turkey, Iran and Pakistan. The entry of the Central Asian republics led some economists to look forward to the formation of an 'Islamic Common Market', covering the enormous territory from the Altai region and the Himalayan mountains to the Indian Ocean and the Mediterranean. Equally unexpected for Russia was the entry of the Central Asian states in 1992 into the CSCE, which had previously kept out of Asia. Delegations from all the republics attracted great attention when they participated in a top-level, heads-of-state meeting of the Islamic Conference Organization which was held in Dakar, Senegal, in December 1991. They also sent delegations to other international religious conferences. Uzbekistan pursued its diplomacy, too, in southeast Asia: President Karimov made an official visit to Malaysia and Indonesia in June 1992, signing among other things an agreement for large-scale credit in Jakarta.

The Russian assumption about the inexperience of the Central Asian governments in international affairs was partly justified. What the Russian leadership failed to appreciate, however, was the extent to which the leaders of these various republics would seek to mount the international stage as a way of strengthening the international authority of their regimes and, at the same time, their own domestic popularity. President Saparmurad Niyazov of Turkmenistan, for example, has recently assumed the title of 'Turkmenbashi' (i.e. 'Leader of all Turkmen'), and reportedly has begun to compare himself with de Gaulle, Bismarck and Ataturk. According to *Le Monde* he was quoted as saying: 'Turkmen have always worshipped something: first fire, then Islam, then Marx ... People need something to believe in ... Today the portraits of Niyazov are necessary so as to convince people of the idea of their independence.'[3]

One sure way for the leaders to increase their popularity was to stress the differences between themselves and Moscow, between the Muslim states of Central Asia on the one hand and the European Christian states on the other. In this respect they very quickly learnt the advantages of playing the card of international politician, even statesman, as a way of keeping opponents on the defensive.

The emphasis on policy differences from Moscow very quickly resulted in changes in the foreign policies of the individual republics as compared with those of the Soviet Union. A closer linkage between the domestic politics of individual Central Asian states and their foreign policies was also established: they did not all march down the same path. This was particularly evident in their relations with Turkey and Iran. Where the predominantly Turkic-speaking republics – Kazakhstan, Uzbekistan and

Turkmenistan – paid great attention to Turkey, with whom they signed wide-ranging political and economic agreements, Tajikistan made Iran its number one priority. It was symptomatic that the then Tajik President Nabiev left Dushanbe at the height of the civil war in early July 1992 to make an official visit to Iran, where he discussed the possibilities of mediation by Tehran in the conflict.

Relations between the Central Asian republics and the outside world thus became much more complex. Perhaps because they were savouring their own independence, their leaders were reluctant to make a common cause too often. For example, at a summit of leaders in the region in Bishkek on 23 April 1992, President Niyazov refused to sign an agreement on economic and financial cooperation. Then at a CIS summit in Tashkent on 15 May 1992 he refused to sign a declaration on collective security and mutual assistance. This was so unexpected that the ITAR-TASS press agency initially reported that he had signed, and it was only on the following day that they were forced to publish his refusal. Sometimes leaders have competed for influence over neighbours. This has been particularly true of President Karimov of Uzbekistan and President Nazarbayev of Kazakhstan.

Nor have the leaders of the states of Central Asia been too willing to sacrifice their political interests for the sake of a broader Islamic front. Under the Soviet system all Islamic clergy in Central Asia were under the authority of the Muslim Board of Central Asia and Kazakhstan in Tashkent. President Nazarbayev believed this might allow politicians outside his republic to interfere in Kazakhstan's internal affairs, and he arranged for clergy in his republic to set up their own independent board.

Russia does of course have basic foreign policy interests in the region, and it cannot simply withdraw. The first is security. The now Christian-oriented Russian government is sensitive to threats of 'Islamic fundamentalism', which makes it especially concerned about its southern frontier. Moscow calculates that it is more convenient to try to control possible infiltration from places such as Afghanistan across the shorter southern borders of the former Central Asian republics than across their much longer boundary with Russia.[4] The second core Russian interest in the region is control of the nuclear weapons that Kazakhstan inherited from the Soviet Union. The third core interest is transport: both ensuring that Russia has unrestricted access to rail links between Europe and Asia, at non-extortionate prices, and trying to ensure that as much trade as possible continues to flow between Europe, the Middle East and the Far East via Russia. Finally, Russia is vitally interested in the fate of Russians living in the neighbouring states of the FSU, Central Asia included.

For all these reasons Russia's relations with Central Asia became much more complex after 1991. It had to deal with independent states which all had, albeit to varying degrees, nationalistic domestic political constituencies which resented Russia's past domination and wanted some kind of compensation. Despite this similarity, however, they could adopt quite different policies towards Russia. Whereas, for example, President Nazarbayev advocated signing the Federal Treaty in 1991, President Karimov was the first to refuse to do so.

This greater variety of foreign policies in the region also complicated Russia's relations with other states towards which Moscow had once had the sole right to determine Soviet policies. For example, whereas previously the USSR had supported India in its dispute with Pakistan over Kashmir, the new Uzbek President Karimov signed an agreement with Prime Minister Nawaz Sharif in June 1992 which effectively supported the Pakistani position over Kashmir. This further cooled relations between New Delhi and Moscow, already damaged by Russia's inability to maintain the FSU's aid policy towards India. It also encouraged India to become more active in Central Asia, as will be discussed in Chapter 5, so as to try to prevent the other republics of the region from following Uzbekistan's example. In turn this means that the possibility of frictions between Indian and Russian foreign policies in the region has increased. The 'Indian factor' in Russian foreign policy towards Central Asia may now have more general repercussions for Russia's relations with India.

If the link between domestic and foreign policies became closer for the Central Asian states after December 1991, the same was true in some respects for Russia as well. Nowhere was this more apparent than in the issue of the status of Russian citizens residing in Central Asia. This is an extremely sensitive issue in Russian politics. Throughout 1992 the nationalist press in Russia regularly printed articles on the exodus of hundreds of thousands of Russians from Central Asia, allegedly as a result of pressure and discrimination from the local authorities. And even though there has not been an aggressive state-directed Islamic movement in Central Asia, the fears of Russians have in general been heightened by the much greater militancy of Islamic clergy in the northern Caucasus. In any case the civil war in Tajikistan has certainly encouraged Russians living in the country to flee, as will be seen below. The issue of the 'Russian-speaking hostages' was widely exploited during the election campaign in Russia in autumn 1993 and contributed in no small way to the success of Zhirinovsky's party. It is also hotly debated in the State Duma.

From Moscow's viewpoint the solution is for the other republics to treat Russians equally in all respects. Moscow's ideal is dual nationality for Russian citizens of other republics. Of course all the leaders of the Central Asian republics are aware of the threat to their regimes and their states posed by ethnic conflict. President Nazarbayev, for example, coined the geographical but non-ethnic term 'Kazakhstaner' for use in the constitution, so as emphasize that land and public property in Kazakhstan belonged to all the people living there, and not just to the dominant racial group. No one, however, was willing to concede the principle of dual nationality until a breakthrough occurred at the Ashkhabad summit of the CIS in December 1993, when President Niyazov announced that Turkmenistan intended to introduce this concept into its legal and political system. According to the correspondent of the Moscow journal *Novoe Vremya*, the effect on President Yeltsin was so moving that he accepted the formal presentation of a passport as a citizen of Turkmenistan. He was advised afterwards that this was unconstitutional for the President of Russia and that he must return it. There are now reports that Kyrgyzstan and Tajikistan are considering following Turkmenistan's example.

Niyazov's action is part of a wider rapprochement between Turkmenistan and Russia. There was also an agreement for the joint stationing of Russian and Turkmen troops to guard the republic's frontiers. In future Russian border guards will be under their own command, and border patrols will be carried out by Turkmen troops under the command of Russian officers who are serving under contract. According to *Le Monde*, Niyazov agreed to the retention in the republic of Russia's ground-tracking station for space flights. Moreover, in December 1993 negotiations began over Russian assistance in establishing a Turkmen navy, which the Russians could use in an emergency, as well as the construction of a Russian naval base in Krasnovodsk (now renamed Turkmenbashi).

These significant concessions made by Turkmenistan reflect the state's increasing economic difficulties. Until now, Ukraine and Uzbekistan have refused to pay for supplies of Turkmenistan gas, which increases the government's losses. Hopes of billions of credits from Saudi Arabia have been dashed. Industry is working part-time.

By contrast, Russia's relations with Uzbekistan worsened at the end of 1993. Primarily this was a consequence of the Tajik civil war.

The Tajik factor
In September 1993 Tajikistan marked the second anniversary of its inde-

pendence. For eighteen months the republic had experienced the most bloody civil war in the history of the republics of the CIS. Over 80,000 people have died, over 800,000 have emigrated to other states of the CIS, and roughly 100,000 have emigrated or been deported to Afghanistan. The republic has lost a significant proportion of its own intelligentsia, as well as around 150,000 Russian-speakers, primarily engineers, technicians and skilled workers. This exodus has brought a number of enterprises to a halt, especially in the mining and energy sectors. Moreover, over 80,000 industrial enterprises have been destroyed. In the south of the republic virtually all housing has been destroyed too. In 1992 and 1993 only 9–10 per cent of the normal crop of cotton was harvested.

Clashes between regions and clans lie at the bottom of the civil war.[5] Although the opposition has been labelled 'Islamicists', 'Islamic extremists', sometimes 'Wahhabis', the religious factor is far from playing the decisive role in the conflict, while the influence of the clergy upon it has in general been exaggerated. Speeches either for or against Islam are only a cover for struggles between the elites of regional clans. Tajikistan is divided into four regions, each separated from the others by mountain ranges. There is no direct railway network linking all of them, and travel from one part to another may require transit through neighbouring states.

The northern part, around Khojent, is adjacent to and inclined towards Uzbekistan. Roughly one-third of the inhabitants there are Uzbeks. Indeed until 1929 Khojent and its environs belonged to Uzbekistan. This has led President Karimov to repeat that the population there wish to return to Uzbekistan, although he personally does not support it. The Pamir region is particularly isolated, being linked with the rest of the republic by one road. Here the population is divided into two unequal halves. Over 80 per cent – highland Tajiks – inhabit the western Pamir region. As mentioned in Chapter 2, they are quite different from other Tajiks in terms of culture, ethnic, linguistic and even religious relations. Whereas the others are Sunnis, the highland Tajiks are Shiite Ismailis. The rest of the population are Kyrgyz. They inhabit the eastern part of the Pamirs and are linked by a mountain road with the Kyrgyz centre of Osh.

Throughout the whole existence of the Tajik republic, power has been in the hands of people from Leninabad province. This led to the uneven economic development of various regions. Most resources were invested in the industrial and cultural development of Dushanbe and Leninabad. In the later years of Soviet rule, significant capital was invested in developing the irrigation system of the fertile lands of Kulyab and

Kurgan-Tyube provinces. This was done on the direct orders of Moscow with the aim of cultivating long-staple cotton, which was extremely important for Soviet textiles. People were resettled in these provinces from the mountain regions so as to develop cotton production. This laid the foundation for the bloody clashes of 1992–3, because of the shortage of fertile plots of land in southern Tajikistan. It should be remembered that 93 per cent of the republic is mountainous. Concerns about the economics, culture and welfare of the highland regions of the Pamirs were the lowest priority. The result was resentment against the 'dominance of the Leninabaders'; the centre of opposition was the city of Garm.

In 1991–2 parties were formed to further the struggle. The leaders of the Garm and Pamir clans formed the Democratic Party of Tajikistan. Almost simultaneously the Islamic Revival Party was set up by the peasants of the border region of Kurgan-Tyube. To safeguard their positions the Leninabad and Dushanbe clans created the so-called Popular Front, an extremely varied organization linking northerners and many *déclassé* elements. They were led by the legendary Sangak Safarov, who had spent 25 years in prison for criminal activity, and his deputy Safarali Kenjaev.

In May 1992 after a long and bloody struggle a bloc of democrats and Muslims was victorious. Safarali Kenjaev was forced to flee the capital in one of the tanks of the 201st Russian division, which had the task of peace-making in the republic. However, the formal leader of the Popular Front, President Nabiev, continued his attempts to prevent a full-scale civil war, trying to achieve a balance between the coalition government, in which the democrats and Islamicists had played a leading role since May 1992, and the Popular Front, which used weapons and other equipment from Uzbekistan to train resistance fighters and organized massacres of the local population in Kurgan-Tyube.

In September 1992 President Nabiev was forced to resign under pressure from the democrats and Islamicists. Attempts to negotiate a resolution of the crisis failed. Blood-letting continued throughout the country, especially in the south. In October 1992 units of the Popular Front headed by Safarali Kenjaev were supplied in Termez (Uzbekistan) not only with machine guns but also with artillery and tanks from the Uzbek high command. They then began an assault on Dushanbe.

The massive supplies of heavy equipment from the Uzbek leadership to a non-governmental organization – the Popular Front of Tajikistan – demonstrate not so much the fear in Tashkent of Islamic fundamentalism, but rather the firm resolve of President Karimov to subordinate the neighbouring republic to his influence. This has had a great impact not merely upon Uzbek–Tajik relations, but also upon relations with Russia. In 1992 a government of national reconciliation was set up, with Emomali Rakhmonov as the new President. In 1993 this government signed its first treaty, one of Friendship and Cooperation – not with Russia but with Uzbekistan. In the mind of President Karimov and his entourage this was intended to help establish control by Tashkent not only over Tajik politics, but also over the whole of the frontier of Afghanistan with Uzbekistan and Tajikistan. This would solidify the position and authority of Uzbekistan throughout the whole region of Central Asia, while at the same time preventing any strengthening of Russian influence in Tajikistan.

Meanwhile the Russian leadership and public opinion followed the course of the civil war in Tajikistan with great concern. They were extremely worried about the fate of the 300,000 Russians living in Tajikistan. By mid-1993 over 200,000 had fled, causing enormous difficulties in Russia, where employment and accommodation are already in short supply. At the same time the possible merging of the conflicts in Afghanistan and Tajikistan, and the possible penetration of Muslim fanatics armed with the latest weapons into Uzbekistan, Kyrgyzstan and Kazakhstan presented a serious danger for the Russian Federation, given that over 15 million Muslims live in the Volga region and the northern Caucasus. There was also the danger of drug-smuggling and gun-running into and through Russia.

Russia could also not fail to pay attention to political changes in the region after 3 January 1993. On that day the leaders of the five Central Asian republics met in Tashkent to sign a joint communiqué, which marked the establishment of the Association of States of Central Asia. Thus a new Muslim, Asiatic political and economic grouping was formed inside the CIS. All of this coincided with a resurgence in the influence of Uzbekistan.

In these circumstances, and after significant hesitations, Moscow decided to support the Rakhmonov regime in Tajikistan not merely through political but also by military means. On 25 May 1993 a Treaty of Friendship, Cooperation and Mutual Assistance was signed between the Russian Federation and Tajikistan. A further seven agreements were signed, regularizing the status and responsibilities of Russian border guards in securing the Afghan–Tajik frontier, although they were strongly criticized in Pakistan, Afghanistan and Iran.

The signing of the Russo-Tajik treaty was not the only cause of discord between Russia and Uzbekistan. On 13 May the influential Moscow newspaper *Nezavisimaya gazeta* published an article by two officials in the Russian Ministry of External Economic Relations, who complained that the new Association of States of Central Asia would harm Russian interests and provoke a negative reaction in the Muslim republics of the Russian Federation. They also alleged that the Association was aimed against the Persian-speaking countries. This article was extremely ill-received in Central Asia, and the treaty with Tajikistan itself met with hostility in Uzbekistan, although it was warmly welcomed by the Russian military. Since then, however, the situation on the Tajik–Afghan frontier has not improved. There have been numerous pitched battles, and the Russian border guards, unused to large-scale engagements, have suffered heavy losses. The Russian Ministry of Defence has been forced to send more and more units to Tajikistan, with heavier weapons.

All of this has exacerbated relations between Russia and Uzbekistan. In December 1993 President Karimov condemned the concept of dual nationality, saying that it would never be introduced in Uzbekistan. Then, when he was criticized for manipulating personnel changes in the Tajik government, Karimov left Ashkhabad so hurriedly that President Niyazov did not have time to see him off at the airport.

Events of 1994
During April 1994 serious changes took place in relations between Russia and the states of Central Asia, first with Uzbekistan and then with Kazakhstan. This was linked with two factors: a decline in the economic situation in Uzbekistan, and a sharp deterioration in the civil war in Afghanistan which threatened to spill over into the civil war in Tajikistan. The Uzbek Afghan General Dostum, a client of Uzbekistan, switched from support for President Rabani to the camp of Hikmatyar, his fiercest enemy – an Islamic fundamentalist, the leader of the Pushtuns, and an advocate of a great nationalist and Islamic-fundamentalist war in Tajikistan. Then Karimov realized that he would be unable solely through his own efforts to preserve either Tajikistan or the Afghan–Uzbek frontier. He changed his economic policies with a decree dated 21 January 1994, which introduced wide-ranging economic liberalization, opened the way for foreign capital investment, allowed private ownership of land for all including foreigners, and allowed unrestricted import and export of foreign currency. All this changed the economic situation, but it was also a signal that Karimov was ready to introduce economic liberalization as Russia had done, instead of holding it back. Indeed Uzbekistan was now one step ahead of Russia.

The situation culminated in a formal state visit by Karimov to Moscow on 2–3 March 1994, during which a number of extremely important agreements were signed. These concerned not merely economic contacts but also military relations. Russia was allowed to retain its military positions in Uzbekistan, and the agreement even envisaged liaison between Russian and Uzbek frontier guards on Afghan territory.

Thus the whole length of the enormous Uzbek frontier with Afghanistan was to a significant extent put under the control of Russia. This was in addition to the frontier between Turkmenistan and Afghanistan, which had been the subject of an earlier agreement between Niyazov and Yeltsin in December 1993 in Ashkhabad.

Moreover, Karimov gave his approval for the government of President Rakhmonov finally to begin negotiations with the Tajik opposition, which was partly in hiding in the Pamirs, and partly in exile in Afghanistan, Iran and Saudi Arabia. In March 1994 the First Deputy Russian Foreign Minister, Anatoly Adamyshin, held talks in Tehran with leaders of the Tajik opposition on the opening of peace talks with the Tajik government. Thus, under the combined pressure of Russia and Uzbekistan, Rakhmonov was obliged to allow an official Tajik government visit (admittedly not at the highest level) to Moscow, where in April 1994 Tajik–Tajik talks began. These talks are as yet far from being concluded, but at least a start has been made. This represents a triumph for Russian foreign policy in its dealings with Central Asia.

Another extremely important event in relations between Russia and Central Asia was the official state visit to Moscow by President Nazarbayev of Kazakhstan at the beginning of April 1994. Agreement was reached on a number of vitally important, difficult issues, including the arrangement for joint use of the Baikonur cosmodrome (which in practice becomes a Russian base on the territory of Kazakhstan), for which Russia will pay Kazakhstan annually not US$7 billion (as stated in earlier press reports) but $115 million. Agreement was also achieved on a number of political, economic and social problems.

This showed that Russia, whose relations with Kazakhstan had worsened at the end of 1993, had fully re-established its position in Almaty. During his visit, President Nazarbayev made a speech at Moscow University to academics and students, in which he outlined the idea of a new Euro-Asian Union linking a number of former Soviet republics, primarily Russia and Kazakhstan, which would form a more stable and robust entity than the CIS. Although the proposal did not receive equivalent support from Moscow, the fact that it was made suggested that Russian policy towards Central Asia had achieved significant success. It is an extremely important factor in international affairs in the region, and this will have a substantial impact upon the situation in Afghanistan as well.

Conclusion: prospects for the relationship
One of the paradoxes about the increasing independence of Central Asia is that there is now a greater equality of interdependence between the region and the Russian Federation. In practice this means that Russia and its government are more dependent than ever before upon Central Asia and what happens there. In the sphere of politics the fate of the Russian minority in the former Soviet Union outside the territory of the Russian Federation is now a subject of fascination for the new political parties in Russia, especially the more nationalistically minded. Were this minority to suffer obvious official discrimination, the temptation for Russian politicians to intervene would become irresistible. The temptation would be particularly acute in this region because of the still widespread phobia of 'Muslim fundamentalism'. Even though the region as a whole may be relatively unlikely to turn to Islamic fundamentalism, especially of an Iranian kind, there is no doubt that Islam now plays a visibly more important role in Central Asian politics and public life than before. The number of functioning mosques in Central Asia grew 150 times between 1987 and 1992, and parties with a strong Islamic identity, such as the Islamic Revival parties of Tajikistan and Uzbekistan, have begun to appear. And in the Fergana valley in Uzbekistan, a centre of Orthodox Islam, the Mufti of Tashkent was nominated for state president.

As many of the peoples who live in Central Asia search for a new identity, the Russian people are confronted by their own crisis of national identity, and they are turning increasingly to Christianity to fill the gap. In these circumstances the Christian/Muslim divide is an issue which can easily provoke an emotional response. In turn this could affect the whole temper of Russian domestic politics.

There are, further, the 15 million Muslim believers inside the Russian Federation. They too are becoming more assertive, and now watch what happens in Central Asia with greater interest. Were there to be a confrontation between Russia and Central Asian states, it could well radicalize the opinions of these Muslims, most of whom are also of Turkic origin. In turn that would certainly antagonize the aggressively Christian believers inside Russia. For Russia the strengthening of Turkey's influence represents a danger, particularly as pan-Turks have developed an interest in their kin inside Russia. Primarily this means Tatars and Bashkirs – and in June 1992 a World Congress of Tatars was held in Kazan'. But pan-Turks have even declared Yakuts to be 'the easternmost Turks', a sentiment which has contributed to the growth of separatism in the Yakut-Sakha Autonomous Republic.

In this sense, therefore, politics in Russia is now at least potentially more vulnerable to political developments in Central Asia and their ramifications than ever before. It also goes without saying that a more stridently nationalist government in Moscow could provoke a more aggressively nationalist response in Central Asia, as well as in other parts of the FSU. In this sense each of the republics of the CIS is more deeply affected by actions taken by the others than was ever the case in the USSR.

Diplomatically Russia is now certainly focusing again upon the importance of good relations with its neighbours in the 'near abroad'. In mid-January 1994 Foreign Minister Kozyrev was reported as telling a conference of Russian ambassadors to the CIS and Baltic states:

> The countries of the CIS and the Baltic are the region where Russia's primary vital interests are concentrated. They are also the source of fundamental threats to those interests ... We must not abandon these regions which have been Russian spheres of interest for centuries. And we must not be afraid of saying this.

Although this statement caused a sensation in the Baltic states, it received great attention in Central Asia as well.

Economically, too, Russia has (re-)discovered its dependence upon Central Asia. This is not just a matter of energy supplies, although those are important. The question of a 'fair' market price for oil and, above all, natural gas has set Turkmenistan against Ukraine. Indeed it was the threat by Turkmenistan to cut off natural gas supplies to Ukraine at the end of 1991 and to divert them to Iran and Turkey that forced Ukraine to accept a rise from the old Soviet price of 3 kopeks per cubic metre to 80 kopeks – which, the Turkmen leaders insisted, was still only half the world price. Indeed for a while Turkmenistan put its threat into effect, thereby straining Russo-Ukrainian relations. Although Turkmenistan had signed an agreement to supply Ukraine with gas, the only way in which it could implement this was by putting the gas into the old trans-Union pipeline which fed the eastern part of Russia, while Russia compensated by sending an equivalent amount of its own gas to Ukraine from a source further west. When Turkmenistan interrupted its supplies to Ukraine, in practice this meant that it cut off supplies to Russian consumers; it was Russia itself that had to implement the cut to Ukraine.

These increases in the price of Central Asian energy supplies have led to repeated decisions by the Russian government to raise the prices charged for energy to consumers. But Central Asia has also raised prices on raw cotton, in part as a reaction against the previously imposed excessive monoculture of cotton. A reduction in the area under cotton cultivation has also led to price increases, which have had to be passed on to Russian factories. The effect upon textile plants, e.g. in Ivanovo province, has been dramatic, causing bankruptcies and unemployment.

Yet the increased dependence and vulnerability have not all worked in one direction. Central Asia too has begun to rediscover the continued importance of good working relations with Moscow. It is true that compared with some regions of the FSU, Central Asia has in general been less inclined to exaggerate the possibilities of independence. All the republics of the region agreed to join the CIS, for example, unlike several other former Soviet republics. Some, especially Turkmenistan, have become vitally aware of the need for Russian assistance in organizing their defence. Yet they did also hope that their rich reserves of minerals and other resources would attract flocks of foreign investors, whose money would liberate their economies from dependence upon Moscow. Reality has failed to match their expectations. Some spectacularly large deals have been struck, such as the US$20 billion Chevron deal for the Tengiz oilfield in Kazakhstan, as well as other deals to exploit energy resources in that republic, involving, for example, British Gas. Other states have offered significant exchange and training programmes for personnel from the governments and for academics. It is also true that projects for expanding the region's transport links with other parts of the world have received a great deal of practical attention. As mentioned above, schemes have been devised to extend existing rail links to other neighbouring states. The gap between the rail lines linking Xinjiang as well as the rest of China with Kazakhstan and the cross-Siberian routes has already been filled, offering the possibility for significant reductions in the time for shipping goods to Europe from eastern China and the Far East generally. Further lines are planned, as well as a pipeline between Kazakhstan and Iranian ports in the Persian Gulf. Their realization would extend the range of options for companies wishing to ship goods between the Far East and Asia, thus further strengthening Central Asia's independence.

Nevertheless, even though foreign capital has been a little more willingly invested in Central Asia than in Russia itself, it cannot be said that the offers of assistance which poured into the region after 1991 have remotely matched the expectations of their leaders. As a result, the republics of Central Asia have seen the need to cooperate with Moscow, albeit to varying degrees. They do not have to climb down humiliatingly as Georgia has had to do. They still have an option for developing economic and other ties.

This is a cooperation which must bring tangible benefits to both sides, for otherwise it will encounter increasing hostility from domestic constituencies in both Russia and the Central Asian republics; the feeling of exploitation is mutual and long-standing. The effect of environmental disasters from the past still needs to be dealt with. Demands that Russia should pay for the costs of cleaning up the nuclear test facilities at Semipalatinsk and the drying-up of the Aral Sea, as well as the salination of water and land caused by unwise land reclamation and irrigation schemes, could easily resurface if economic conditions worsen, precisely at a time when Russian agreement would be even less likely. Under those conditions political relations could rapidly plummet.

But just in case economic relations with Russia fail to bring the expected benefits, the agreement of the leaders of the Central Asian republics to begin to inject some content into their concept of an Islamic common market or free trade area in December 1993 represents at the very least an insurance policy. Although there may be significant potential rivalry between the various republics, since many of their economic strengths and resources overlap rather than complement each other, nonetheless this attempt at economic cooperation might at least mitigate the more severe damage caused by any rift with Moscow. The fact that the Tashkent Declaration could be signed by both President Nazarbayev, who was one of the chief architects of the CIS, and President Karimov, who has never shown great sympathy for Russia or its peace-making mission in Central Asia, shows that options are being kept open, whatever happens in Russia.

4

THE MIDDLE EAST AND CENTRAL ASIA

Philip Robins

Introduction

The modern state system of the Middle East[1] was created in the aftermath of the First World War. This period coincided with the forcible reintegration of part of Central Asia into the newly created centralized authoritarian state of the Soviet Union. Therefore, by the time newly independent state actors had begun to emerge in the Middle East, the region we now know as the former Soviet Central Asia was already off limits. In short, although some states of the Middle East have enjoyed an independent existence for some 70 years, they have had little to do with the political entities and societies of the newly emerged Central Asian republics.

It is only since 1985, with Gorbachev's assumption of power and the advent of glasnost, that an emerging interaction has taken place between the Central Asian republics and the states of the Middle East. During these early years, interaction occurred only on a small scale and was low-key in nature. Relations with Moscow continued to dominate bilateral ties between the USSR and the Middle Eastern states, friends and foes alike. Since the political elites in Central Asia were more content with the Union than their Slavic counterparts, and the Middle Eastern states were preoccupied with the superpower status of the USSR, there was little attempt to develop genuine bilateral relations. Even during much of 1991 with the Soviet Union in terminal decline, when the Central Asian states were belatedly seeking to develop their own set of foreign relations, the Middle Eastern states as a whole were wary of such overtures for fear of offending Moscow.[2] It is therefore only largely since the break-up of the USSR at the end of 1991 that the Middle East and former Soviet Central Asia have begun to interact freely.

Given the paucity of earlier contacts between the two regions, the most important characteristic of the relationships which have begun to emerge over the past three years is the lack of ballast – that is to say, the lack of the necessary accumulation of personal and official contacts, together with the experience of economic and political interaction, to provide stability and continuity. As a result, the relationships among the states from the two regions have been prey to misunderstanding and misconception. They have been characterized by curiosity rather than an accurate perception of common interest; by unrealistic expectation, often followed by deep disappointment.

It is therefore likely to be some time before clear and stable trends emerge in the nature of the relationships between Middle Eastern states and the new republics of Central Asia. Moreover, given the uncertain relations among and within the states of the former USSR, it is even difficult to estimate what constraints might exist on the sovereignty of these new republics. Against the backdrop of these possible constraints, this chapter will concentrate on the opportunities which Central Asia seems to present, as perceived from a Middle Eastern perspective. First, however, an examination of the two regions will be offered principally from a systemic point of view, highlighting the common features of the two regions. Only then can the emerging nature of relations between the two groups of countries be discussed.

Is Central Asia an extension of the Middle East?

Since the break-up of the Soviet Union it has become fashionable for commentators on the Middle East to speak of Central Asia as having been subsumed within their region. Such a contention has a seductive ring, especially for those who do not approach the Middle East in Arabcentric terms. But is such a description really valid given what has already been said about the lack of ballast in the relationship? Indeed, is such a description at all helpful in analysing the political and other relations between the two regions? The latter question is particularly important from the point of view of scholarly inquiry. Two potential distortions can easily lead from an acceptance of this premise: first, a tendency to exaggerate the impact of the Middle East on Central Asia; and, second, the treatment of Central Asia as a largely passive area, subject to the impact of the Middle East, but itself having little impact in return.

The state system

The state systems of the Middle East and Central Asia are indeed very similar in character. If the Middle East can be succinctly described as a system of 'small states', poorly consolidated, with strong competing claims on the loyalty of the population in rivalry to the state, such a description fits the Central Asian system almost as well.

These common characteristics are likely to give rise to a number of similar problems in the intraregional politics of the two areas. Two examples will suffice to illustrate the point. The first is the arbitrary nature of the states that have been created and the often widespread territorial disputes among these states. In both the Middle East and Central Asia the present state system was not drawn up as a result of indigenous activity, let alone consensus, but was largely imposed by colonial diktat. In the Middle East the old colonial powers of Britain and France were mainly responsible for the creation of new states; for Central Asia it was the new Soviet state with its centre of power in Moscow that subdivided the region. In both cases territory was allocated according to the criteria of the dominant metropolitan powers rather than those of the communities that would have to live with such borders. The decision to include the Tajik cities of Bukhara and Samarkand in Uzbekistan was consequently as controversial as was, for instance, the inclusion of the vilayet of Mosul in Iraq or the separation of Transjordan from Palestine.[3] These central questions of the contested nature of the state system and the arbitrary nature of territorial allocation have in turn led to a number of other problems, such as the existence of minority populations within states and numerous border disputes. It is these latter questions that are most likely to be a source of tension in both regions today.

The second example is the vulnerability which almost inevitably accompanies the creation of states with small populations and little sense of territorial state nationalism. Such states are immediately susceptible to the intrusive interference of larger neighbouring states. They may even be subject to occupation by their larger neighbours. In the Middle East, the invasion of Kuwait by Iraq is an example of such a phenomenon at its crudest; the occupation of much of Lebanon by Syria and of the southern-most part of that country by Israel would also fall into the same category. In Central Asia, the continued presence of Russian forces in many of the southern republics is not dissimilar.

But does this similarity between the problems confronting the two regions have implications for the relations between them, or is it little more than an interesting observation which would apply equally well if

Central Asia were compared, for instance, with black Africa? This will depend on the degree and frequency of interaction between the two regions, and on perceptions of mutual utility. The greater the interaction, the greater the chance that the states of one area will become drawn into the tensions and manoeuvrings of the other. This involvement will be heightened if one faction or government perceives it as advantageous to develop political resources in states of the other region.

To date, the best example of this phenomenon has taken place elsewhere within the former Soviet southern belt, namely in the Caucasus. In this area, which is more geographically proximate to the Middle East, both Turkey and Iran have perceived important interests to be at stake in relation to the conflict between Armenia and Azerbaijan. The role of Iran in particular has been instructive. First Iran tilted in the direction of Armenia for fear of the growth of Azerbaijani nationalism, which it was felt could have a disruptive influence on the stability and integrity of Iran. Then it revised its stance as it attracted large numbers of Azerbaijani refugees after the Armenians' battlefield victories, as well as provoking the disquiet of its own public opinion. It should be noted that this was an important case of the politics and instability of the former Soviet Union affecting the politics of Iran, rather than a situation where the Middle Eastern state was the actor and the Caucasian states were cast in a passive role. Most significantly, it shows the impact which an unstable state subsystem can have on an adjoining state not usually identified as being part of that subsystem. Moreover, it also shows that a political crisis in one weak, fragmented international state system can easily reverberate on a neighbouring one.

While it would seem a good bet that the Caucasus will continue to be an important policy focus for Iran and Turkey, the nature of the impact of Central Asia on the politics of the Middle East and vice versa remains to be seen.

Political culture
There are also similarities between the two regions in the nature of the states themselves and the way they operate. These similar characteristics may be subsumed under the general title of political culture. In order to illustrate the point, three characteristics will be discussed here: the primacy of substate patterns of allegiance; the widespread existence of corruption and nepotism; and the centralized, authoritarian nature of government.

One of the key reasons for the limited nature of the consolidation of the state systems in the Middle East and Central Asia is the continued existence of other substate patterns of loyalty. In both regions tribal and regional loyalties remain extremely strong, usually exerting a greater gravitational pull on the loyalty of individuals than their allegiance to the state. The inability of the state to develop a basis of citizenship which can be embraced by its whole population, combined with its failure to act impartially (for instance through the implementation of a neutral legal system), means that the individual cannot afford to depend on the state. Instead, only by being part of influential communities, whether tribally, confessionally or regionally based, can the individual achieve a reliable level of both protection and access to resources.

The most graphic and certainly the most bloody example of the partial nature of allegiance was the civil war in Tajikistan in the latter half of 1992. As was stressed in the preceding chapter, nominally the civil war was cloaked in an ideological conflict, with the former communists locked in a struggle for power with an alliance of democrats and Islamists. In reality, it was a struggle for supremacy between the regions, in which the north in the form of Leninabad, which had traditionally supplied the rulers of the state during the communist period, defeated the forces from around Kulyab which sought to supplant them. A similar struggle, though without the violence, is taking place in Kazakhstan, where the Great Horde, which enjoyed political dominance during the communist era, is trying to ensure that it retains power in the face of opposition from other clans.[4] In the Middle East, civil wars, notably in South Yemen in 1986 and at different times in Lebanon, often assume ideological clothing, but in reality represent a struggle for power among clans and confessional groupings. Similarly, regionally based government like that witnessed in Tajikistan has its Middle Eastern equivalent in the profile of officials from the Tikrit region in the present Iraqi regime.

Individuals in states in both the Middle East and Central Asia identify frequently with a region, tribe or confessional group. Access to public-sector employment, state services and a notable or shaikh-like figure capable of taking up individual problems with central government all help to make such substate loyalties rational for the individual. In turn, traditional leaders or those who aspire to play a leadership role have to dispense such favours to potential and existing supporters in order to forge and consolidate a power base. They stand to benefit from a loyalty which is extended to them on a personal basis, for being the figure within the larger grouping that has been successful in delivering such resources. Nepotism and corruption are therefore easily justified in local political terms.

Such phenomena are by no means an exclusive product of the post-communist republics of Central Asia, having prevailed in such entities during the Soviet era. What appears to have happened, however, is that this kind of corruption has increased dramatically since the emergence of these entities as independent states. Assuming such an observation is true – and it is largely based on an ever-expanding body of anecdotal evidence – the explanation appears to lie in local factors, with the withering of the Soviet state and the decline of the influence of Moscow. In the Middle East, corruption and nepotism are endemic. Nor are they confined to the Arab world. In Iran, in contrast to the promises of Islamist movements elsewhere in the region, corruption has grown under the mullahs' rule. Even in Turkey, where the political culture is different from the rest of the Middle East, corruption, particularly in local government, is a continuing phenomenon.

The tendency towards centralized, authoritarian politics in the Central Asian and Middle Eastern states is as strong as the tendency towards corruption and nepotism. It is also as rational. Both proceed from the weakness of the state system, with its fragmented political communities and the contested nature of the territorial states that exist. If substate loyalties are stronger than allegiance to the state, and if access to political power carries with it the reward of the disproportionate allocation of jobs and resources to one's supporters, then it is little wonder that the desire for power is intense. Power itself is centralized, both to maximize its benefits and to increase the chances of retaining it. In the absence of any institutional framework for regulating the competition for power, those who aspire to hold power look for other means to realize their ambitions. It is at such a point that the use of violence to achieve power becomes attractive as an option. From the point of view of a regime, the control of coercive and intelligence mechanisms is regarded as paramount for the retention of power. Such mechanisms are then expanded in both size and function to increase their effectiveness and reward their loyalty.

In Central Asia there has also been a noticeable increase in authoritarianism since the breakdown of the Soviet state. The security and intelligence apparatuses, which existed during Soviet times, have been rejuvenated. Only in Kyrgyzstan is it debatable whether there has been an increase in authoritarianism since 1991.

As with Central Asia today, centralization and authoritarianism have long been characteristics of Middle East states. In the Gulf states such a trend has been prevalent since those in power acquired access to extensive oil wealth, which enabled them to abandon the more balanced system of political relations that had prevailed before. Authoritarianism was elevated to the level of an art form by the radical regimes in power in Iraq and Syria from the 1960s onwards. Even in countries which have undertaken democratic experiments recently, the centralization of power has continued, either in stark terms as in Algeria, or more subtly, as in Jordan and Kuwait. Revolutionary Iran has seen the concentration of power in the hands of the Islamic regime, while those outside certain ideological parameters are effectively excluded from political participation. Turkey has suffered the periodic intervention of the military in government; today the armed forces exert considerable influence behind the scenes, especially in regard to official responses to the Kurdish insurgency in the southeast of the country. In all the countries of the Middle East, including Israel, there exist well-developed and powerful security and intelligence services, with only limited transparency and processes of accountability to keep them in check.

Religion and language
When the Central Asian republics together with Azerbaijan began to emerge as independent entities, there was a tendency on the part of many commentators to emphasize the common characteristics between them and the states of the Middle East. These observations were not made on the basis of common systemic attributes or similarities of political culture, but on the perception of a common religion, culture and language. The common religious bond was that of Islam, though differences between Sunni and Shia Islam were noted. With regard to language, the common denominator was that of the Turkic linguistic family. Clearly there are religious and linguistic commonalities between the Middle East and Central Asia. However, the emphasis placed on such links was invariably based on meagre information, and tended to exaggerate the importance of such ties. Furthermore, it tended to be assumed that a common religious and linguistic bond would automatically result in the creation of a common political bond.

Arguably, the issue of religion has involved the greatest distortion. Middle Eastern studies have been subject to a major debate for the past decade and a half over the issue of 'Orientalism'.[5] One of the key problems with the 'Orientalist' view is the reductionist importance it ascribes to the Islamic religion. Rather than the Islamic world being made subject to the general social analysis that would be applied to other regions of the globe, 'Orientalism' regards the Islamic religion as producing a unique pattern of behaviour which defies such general approaches. The opening-up of Central Asia has resulted in some elementary 'Orientalist' conclusions about its nature, as if the debate in the Middle East context had not taken place. At the forefront of these misconceptions is the reduction of the Central Asian republics to what is perceived as their religious identity: the Central Asian states are Muslim, *ergo* they must gravitate towards a Muslim community of states.

Such crude views as these inevitably obscure the nature of Islam in Central Asia, and indeed the religious composition of these new states in general and its political significance. It is highly debatable whether a state like Kazakhstan can be described as being 'Muslim' at all, given that its Muslim population constitutes less than 50 per cent of its inhabitants. By contrast, in the Middle East it is highly unusual to refer to any of the region's countries as 'Muslim states', let alone those such as Lebanon which have a significant Christian minority.

In any case, Islam in Central Asia was remarkably free of dogma and discipline during the Soviet period, with a high degree of ignorance surrounding what for Middle Eastern Muslims would be regarded as religious orthodoxies.[6] At least up to the present, much of Central Asia has taken a rather relaxed approach towards the Islamic religion, and to political Islam in particular. This represents a marked difference from the contemporary Middle East on both counts.

With respect to language, many of the same observations apply. Language does not by itself inform a whole series of cultural values, let alone political orientations. The fact that, for example, residents of Turkey and Kazakhstan speak a variant of the same language does not mean anything more profound than that there is likely to be some limited form of mutual identification. Thus, language need not necessarily be more important as a common characteristic than any other criteria from geopolitics to youth culture.

As with Islam, the simple existence of a common linguistic origin has been elevated to such a height as to mask other important linguistic differences. Thus, while the Turkish of Anatolia and the language spoken in Azerbaijan are close and just about mutually intelligible, the Turkish of Anatolia and the Turkic language of the Kazakhs or the Kyrgyz are very different indeed, so much so that a Turk wanting to be easily understood in Kazakhstan or Kyrgyzstan needs some three to four months of intensive study. With the elite of the Central Asian republics usually more comfortable with Russian, ironically communication between Turkish and Central Asian officials often takes place in Russian via an interpreter.

Mindful of the fact that language is a political as well as a cultural resource, the government of Turkey has eagerly pursued the Central Asian republics to try to persuade them to abandon Cyrillic in favour of the Latin script. Such a goal has been surprisingly difficult to realize if one takes at face value the claims that have been made for the importance of language. While Azerbaijan has formally accepted the adoption of the Latin alphabet, the other republics are at varying stages of procrastination over the issue of language reform. In view of the fact that the Latin script has the additional attraction of being used by business, diplomacy and international institutions, the pulling power of the Turkic family of languages would not appear to be particularly strong. Once again, the reasons for resisting such change are entirely understandable. The existence of large Russian minorities, for whom Cyrillic is a key test of their status, the political importance of the Russian Federation, the cost and the practical unpreparedness for reform have all acted as a brake on the rapid implementation of change. Indeed, as noted in Chapter 2, it is by no means certain that the states will implement these changes at all.

Geopolitics

The emergence of Central Asia as a discrete area for study is an adventure for all, analysts and academics alike, apart from a handful of linguists and anthropologists who have ploughed this particular furrow for many years. In view of this general ignorance of Central Asia it is a useful exercise to include an appraisal of geography in the relations between this region and its neighbours. Even a cursory look at a map of Central Asia will show that while it can be said that the Middle East is a region adjacent to former Soviet Central Asia, only Iran among the regional states provides actual geographical contiguity. Moreover, even if Azerbaijan is included alongside Central Asia, it is still only Iran that provides a territorial connection with the Middle East. The failure to appreciate this simple geography is to distort expectations and underestimate the obstacles to a wider relationship between the two regions.

For instance, when the Soviet Union formally broke up, exaggerated claims were immediately made as to the role which Turkey could play in Central Asia. Such claims owed more to ideology than to practicality. The major proponent of such a view was the United States, which feared that a political vacuum had been created in Central Asia and that it would be filled by Iran and its revolutionary brand of Islam. In a somewhat hurried attempt to ensure that this did not happen, Washington urged Turkey to fill this vacuum first. US thinking therefore owed more to the old Cold War paradigm of bipolar, zero-sum competition than it did to the new realities on the ground.

The US view was right in one sense, though for the wrong reason. Iran was clearly well placed to develop close relations with the southern part of the former Soviet Union. However, the reason for this was its geographical proximity, not its revolutionary ideology. Indeed, the latter, together with the American reaction, has proved to be an obstacle for Iran in developing relations with the new republics, though one which geography appears finally to have surmounted.[7]

The US view with respect to Turkey has since been exposed as being informed in part by wishful thinking. Turkey has encountered serious geographical problems as it has tried to develop relations with Central Asia. These have principally related to issues of access. The unrest in Georgia and the war in Azerbaijan have made road communications between Turkey and Central Asia precarious. Iran has periodically disrupted Turkey's road access to Central Asia,[8] thereby (whether consciously or otherwise) drawing attention to its own more favourable location. Turkey has tried to neutralize this disadvantage of geography. It has sought to develop non-terrestrial communications, putting emphasis on the development of a modern telecommunications network, and encouraging air transport routes. These have, however, done little to compensate for Turkey's precarious lines of land communications.

The lack of geographical access to Central Asia is compounded by the lines of existing infrastructure. These were developed during the period of Soviet rule and consequently were aimed at integrating Central Asia into the rest of the Soviet state. Infrastructural lines therefore tend to run in a northerly direction. This obviously orientates the Central Asian republics away from the Middle East, with which there was little trade during the Soviet period. There now exists one Eurasian rail link which reaches Turkey via a ferry across the Caspian Sea. Nevertheless the inadequate infrastructural network connecting Central Asia with the Middle East means that, almost regardless of desire, economic expansion will be severely hampered over the medium term. The prospects for closer economic relations between the two regions over the long term will in turn depend upon whether sizeable infrastructural investment is made in the present. Not surprisingly, much of the tangible progress that is taking place on this front is between the only two contiguous neighbours in the two regions, with a rail link between Turkmenistan and Iran due now to be finished by 1996.

Nevertheless, despite the limited geographical opportunities for interaction between Central Asia and the Middle East, there is one area where cooperation is highly likely. This relates to the one valuable resource that can be found in relative abundance across part of Central Asia, namely hydrocarbons. Kazakhstan and Azerbaijan seem set to emerge as the two main exporters of crude oil; Turkmenistan has extensive reserves of gas, while Uzbekistan has more modest oil reserves. Hitherto, such opportunities have either been neglected, partly for technical reasons, or not been properly exploited for commercial benefit. The new republics of Azerbaijan, Kazakhstan and Turkmenistan in particular are concentrating on trying to harness this resource. Foreign oil companies have been invited in and new pipelines to export these hydrocarbons are being contemplated. The Middle East appears bound to have a role as a conduit for export, especially if Europe emerges as a leading market for such energy. Iran and Turkey are set to be important beneficiaries in the region, by virtue of their location along potential supply routes, although the exact number and course of the expected pipelines have still to be decided.

The Middle East in Central Asia

Having compared the nature of the two regions, I now propose to examine the way in which the leading states of the Middle East perceive new opportunities to have been provided by the opening-up of former Soviet Central Asia. Once again, it is necessary to include the caveat that analysis of such interaction can be based only on a very short period of time. Given this reservation, I would tentatively argue that the interests of the Middle East states fall into three categories: new political resources; a new focus for ideological competition; and a basket of new economic opportunities.

New political resources

The Middle East is not Europe. While the latter concerns itself with humanistic notions of shared rights among peoples, the former is preoccupied with power. While the latter is moving in the direction of shared sovereignty, the former witnesses a continuing struggle to realize and assert sovereignty. At the territorial state level in the Middle East the struggle for consolidation and even survival continues. In order to survive and prosper, states are engaged in an endless round of manoeuvring, each with the objective of maximizing its influence through the cementing of tacit and formal alliances in order to neutralize or undermine the influence of states perceived to be strategic enemies or rivals.

65

The arena for this activity has in the past been confined to the Middle East, for two reasons. First, the boundary of the old Soviet Union had provided a rigid framework which helped to contain such political jockeying. The demise of the USSR and the removal of the frame within which this *modus operandi* was contained offered the possibility that the successor states of the old Soviet Union could be drawn into the Middle East pattern of interstate alliance-making. Second, the fragmentation of the Arab world, together with its own self-preoccupation, had absorbed the Arab states. Not surprisingly, therefore, it has been the non-Arab states of the Middle East, that is to say Israel, Iran and Turkey, that have been the quickest and most enthusiastic to propose relations with the new republics of the former Soviet south.

The motives of these three countries in exploring the potential for new ties with Central Asia are varied, but all are driven first and foremost by political considerations. For *Israel* this new push has been motivated by the Arab–Israeli conflict. Israel is a small state, surrounded on three sides by Arab peoples that at various times have been committed to the eradication of the Jewish state. In the 1950s Israel developed the 'periphery' strategy of making common cause with other Middle Eastern states that, as David Ben-Gurion put it, lay beyond the 'Arab fence'.[9] Israel sought to generate a pact consisting of Turkey, Iran and Ethiopia. This policy was only partially successful, and was finally undermined by the fall of the Shah of Iran. By then, Israel had developed a new strategy to divide the Arab world, an approach which was ultimately successful with the conclusion of a separate peace with Egypt.

The continued formal hostility of the rest of the Arab world, together with the cool nature of the bilateral peace with Egypt, meant that Israel continued to feel embattled. The benefit of peace with Egypt had been in part cancelled out by the antipathy of the Islamic Republic of Iran, which remains ideologically committed to the destruction of Israel. In addition to its residual instinct of peripheralism, Israel now became keen to establish relations with other countries populated principally by Muslims. To do so would show that Israel could coexist normally with Muslim peoples, and would blunt any attempts by Iran to rally the Islamic world against Israel. The emergence of the new republics of Central Asia therefore gave Israel the opportunity to establish political relations with what it perceived as 'Muslim states'.[10] Moreover, the new situation offered the possibility of relations with republics which were largely unaffected either by political Islam or by the Arab–Israeli issue.

For *Turkey*, the chief motivation for wanting to develop political ties with Central Asia was its perception of its own isolation and the unreliability of its allies. Until the break-up of the Soviet Union Turkey was the only state populated primarily by Turks. As such, it did not easily fit into a broader community of states, as the individual Arab territorial states may be said to belong to the Arab world. This sense of isolation was compounded by a perceived historical experience of rejection and betrayal at the hands of supposed friends. This began with the break-up of the Ottoman empire and the attempt by the Entente powers to establish a truncated Turkish state in parts of Anatolia, a plan which was enshrined in the Treaty of Sèvres in 1920. It was only through the efforts of the Turks themselves that this plan was thwarted and the spatial dimension of the modern Turkish state was created. Since then there have been periodic examples of the unreliability of Turkey's allies, notably the 'Johnson letter' affair in 1964, when the US brought pressure to bear on Turkey in order to influence its policy towards Cyprus. The most recent example of this tendency is the European Community's Opinion on Turkey's application for full membership, delivered in December 1989: the EC deferred any consideration of the application and was clearly unenthusiastic. The state of the Turkish psyche has been summed up by Turks in the phrase 'The Turk has no other friend than the Turk'.[11]

The emergence of a belt of what Turks tend to call 'Turkic republics' running from Azerbaijan across Central Asia raised hopes that at last a natural constituency of states had emerged to which Turkey could feel it belonged. The Turkic nature of these republics would not only end the isolation of Turkey but also provide additional cement, thereby consolidating the mutual loyalty of these states. While the Turkish government protested that it would not act as a 'big brother', its self-perception of superiority in the structure of its economy and the working of its democracy suggested that Ankara envisaged exercising a leadership role over these new republics. The prospect must have been attractive: in addition to the psychological boost that such a community of states would have given, Turkey would have expected practical support over a range of issues at international forums, beginning with the Cyprus question.

Iran's motivation for wanting to develop new political relationships in Central Asia stemmed both from its own isolation and from the fact that its geopolitical location actually makes it a player in the Central Asian subsystem of states. Iran's isolation in the Middle East is due to a mixture of ethnic, confessional and strategic elements, compounded by ideology. Even under the Shah, it was perceived by much of the Arab world as a Persian, Shiite regional power that potentially or actually threatened Arab interests in the Persian Gulf. The overthrow of the Shah and the establishment of an assertive regime espousing anti-Western, Islamic radicalism gave a new edge to this traditional suspicion of Iran. The war with Iraq, Iran's attempts to destabilize the smaller Gulf states and the targeting of Kuwaiti shipping from autumn 1986 through to the end of the Iran–Iraq war underlined this perception of Iran as a dangerous, revisionist power. The defeat of Iraq, the traditional counterweight to Iran, in 1991, together with Iran's efforts at rearming and its attempts to gain complete control of the strategic island of Abu Musa, once more raised anxieties about Iran which were shared by the United States, Israel, the Arab Gulf states and Egypt. With virtually no friends in the Middle East, Iran has turned towards Central Asia. Consequently, Tehran has been the main force within the Economic Cooperation Organization both for that body's rejuvenation and for the admission of the Central Asian republics and others as members.

As well as seeking new friends and partners, Iran has been keen to develop political relations in this area because of its own geopolitical location. It has already suffered directly because of instability in the wider area of Central Asia. The two million Afghan refugees who have sought refuge in Iran for well over a decade have been an economic burden. Their presence has helped to make Iran a significant player in the Afghan civil war. The influx of smaller numbers of refugees from the war in Azerbaijan has also underlined the importance of Iran in the Caucasus. These two examples indicate that the problems which have engulfed its northern borders do not allow Tehran the luxury of disengagement. Iran's location next to Turkmenistan makes the establishment of close political relations with its one ex-Soviet Central Asian neighbour very desirable. The connection between rival factions in Afghanistan and the various forces engaged in the Tajik civil war has resulted in Iran becoming a potential, albeit an equivocal, player in Tajikistan.

Ideological competition

In the Middle East ideological divisions, especially those relating to religion, run deep and are a source of enduring tension. Arguably, the two most important ideological divisions in the contemporary Middle East are between secularism and political Islam, and between 'Wahhabism'[12] and the Twelver Shiite version of revolutionary Islam. The secularist–Islamist dichotomy is a philosophical and political debate which may be found across the region. In state terms, the secularist trend is usually associated with Turkey, the one country in the region populated principally by Muslims which is avowedly secular. On the other hand, a number of Middle Eastern regimes base their right to rule on Islam. These include Saudi Arabia and Iran. Both stoutly resist the secularist philosophical tendency. Both have sought to re-Islamize Turkey: Saudi Arabia through the dispersal of funds for mosque-building and religious education, Iran through sedition. One must, however, be careful in ascribing ideological motives to states. In political terms Saudi Arabia and Turkey are close, despite their ideological differences; relations between Iran and Turkey are mercurial, though as much owing to competing interests and a legacy of bad relations as to ideology.

The Wahhabi–Twelver Shiite division is much more specific than the secularist–Islamist cleavage. The Wahhabi sect is a root-and-branch movement of Sunni Islam which is most notably active in Saudi Arabia, where it underpins the political power of the al-Saud family. The Wahhabis are strongly committed to evangelism within the Muslim world, and have been particularly active in Pakistan and Afghanistan. They view the Shiites with great suspicion, and many of them openly claim that Shiites, many of whom live in eastern Saudi Arabia, cannot be considered to be Muslims. Iran is the stronghold of Twelver Islam, which has been radicalized through the revolution and the teaching of Ayatollah Khomeini. The religious community in Iran has also been active in disseminating its ideas in Pakistan and Afghanistan. This ideological competition between the religious establishment in both countries is overlaid by the interstate competition between Saudi Arabia and Iran, which has sharpened since the Islamic revolution. Over a whole series of important issues, from oil policy to relations with the United States, the two governments find themselves at odds.

For ideologists of all four competing views, Central Asia is perceived as a blank canvas. To varying degrees all have felt the urgent need to apply their paint before that of their ideological rivals covers the canvas. The Turkish government has put itself forward as a model for the new republics, placing emphasis on secularism alongside democracy and free market economics. Saudi Arabia and the rest of the Gulf Cooperation Council decided soon after the break-up of the Soviet Union that they would allocate the US$3 billion in aid promised to the USSR for its help during the Gulf crisis exclusively to the republics of Central Asia.[13] By spring 1992 Saudi Arabia was estimated to have invested $1 billion of this figure in Central Asia, much of it in the form of Islamic studies centres and efforts to promulgate the use of the Arabic language.[14] While Iran has generally played down its ideological involvement in Central

Asia in favour of cultural and economic ties, it has not been completely idle in the religious sphere, especially in Tajikistan. By the time of the Tajik civil war Iran was reported as wielding 'significant influence over [Haji Akbar] Turajonzoda', the spiritual leader of the Tajiks.[15]

Although ideological competition is an important factor in relations between Central Asia and the Middle East, there has been a tendency for some to exaggerate its importance hitherto. As already mentioned, the US Secretary of State, James Baker, foresaw the need for Turkey, with its secular model of government, to insert itself into Central Asia first before the Islamist revolutionaries from Iran could win the new republics for radicalism. Baker's obsession became particularly clear during his February 1992 visit to Central Asia. Although he met with some limited success in instilling an initial caution in the approach of the new republics towards Tehran, he misjudged the mood in Central Asia. The governments of the new republics resented his fixation and his consequent lack of interest in their more mundane economic problems. Indeed, Baker made the mistake of thinking that the 'Great Game' could be replicated substituting middle powers for great powers.

The reality has been what one Turkish politician has referred to as 'silent competition'.[16] The competition has existed: for instance, as Turkey has campaigned for the Central Asian states to abandon Cyrillic in favour of the Latin alphabet and Iran has advocated the Arabic script; but the two countries have not turned this competition into a bare-knuckled struggle. The probable reason for this has been that Turco-Iranian bilateral relations are often too tense and delicately poised to risk them spinning out of control by unrestrained competition in Central Asia. Indeed, were the two to become locked in a conflict by proxy in Central Asia it would presumably be to the detriment of both, certainly in economic terms. Furthermore, both Iran and Turkey have come to realize their own limitations with respect to Central Asia, especially with regard to forming a centre of economic gravity for the region. Unlike Baker, both seemed to understand that other neighbouring states, not least Russia, would exert an important influence on Central Asia.

Indeed, the two states have worked hard to try to contain or at least manage this competitive edge. The decision to admit the Central Asian states to membership of the ECO was highly significant in this regard. It marked an end to any illusions that Ankara or Tehran might have had about establishing a zone of influence to the exclusion of the other. The admission of the Central Asian states to the organization virtually guaranteed that both Iran and Turkey would continue to have diplomatic and economic access to the new republics. The hope of advocates of the ECO was that all sides would benefit by increased economic coordination and cooperation.

The trends of the past two years are of course no guarantee as to the future. There are those within Iran who have more ideological aims in mind in the enlargement and reinvigoration of the ECO, namely the creation of a new organization in the Islamic world capable of linking up a number of disparate regions.[17] Afghanistan has already served as an arena for competition, periodically involving violence, between the proponents of Wahhabism and of Twelver Shiism and their supporters. Parts of former Soviet Central Asia could yet prove literally to be a battleground for competing ideologies from the Middle East.

Economic opportunities

Undoubtedly, one of the chief reasons why Central Asia was of immediate interest to a number of states across the Middle East was the perception that there might be economic opportunities to exploit there. Enthusiastic but vague talk about abundant hydrocarbon reserves, together with gold and other minerals, excited expectations of rapid economic growth and business opportunities. Businessmen interested in quick returns tended to be the first to arrive. Unrealistic hopes quickly led to disappointment and even bitterness. These exaggerated expectations were soon dampened when it became clear that there would be a lengthy lead-time before these hydrocarbon reserves could be fully exploited. Payments problems have in turn come to restrict economic potential.

Against this more realistic backdrop, economic interaction between the Middle East and Central Asia has been patchy. Furthermore, it has been restricted to a small group of countries with a comparative advantage in connection with Central Asia. For Israel this advantage has been both demographic and technical – the former relating to the Jewish communities resident in Central Asia,[18] and the latter to the possession of specialist technology and expertise, especially in the water and agricultural sectors, which are sought across Central Asia. For Iran, the comparative advantage has been its geographical proximity, while Turkey's has been broadly economic, especially the competitive nature of its large contracting and trading companies.

Arguably it is *Israel*'s involvement that has been most cost-effective. The Israeli government has taken a strategic decision to forge links with the large mineral-rich republics in particular, in order to position itself for longer-term benefits, both economic and political. It has focused on those areas where Israel has special skills and technology to offer, including such activities as agriculture, hydrology and water management. In doing so, Israel has used its political contacts to enter into a joint approach with the United States towards the Central Asian republics. The two countries have been particularly active in the area of agricultural aid.[19] Israel has therefore achieved an impact greater than its size or resource base would have indicated.[20]

The Israeli government has also been active in encouraging the newly invigorated private sector to pursue opportunities in Central Asia, backing such an effort with material support. The private sector has responded to such a lead. By spring 1992, for example, 18 Israeli companies had visited Kazakhstan alone, with three already 'doing serious business'.[21] At the end of the year the Eisenberg Group, one of Israel's largest and best-known companies, signed a $160 million agreement with Kazakhstan to make and install irrigation equipment,[22] while also holding letters of intent from the republic to the tune of $2 billion.[23] The deal was testimony to the persistence of the company, which had only a month before pulled out of Tajikistan owing to the civil war.[24] By the end of 1992 Israel was the Middle Eastern state with the largest number of joint ventures in Central Asia.[25]

Iran lacks this sort of complementarity with Central Asia. Despite the bullish rhetoric at the governmental level, private sources have always been less sanguine about economic prospects for Iran in Central Asia. It is pointed out that Central Asia has a pressing need for access to foreign capital and contacts with international business, two areas in which Iran's need is also acute.[26] Nor is Iran in a position to be a major aid donor to Central Asia. Tehran's parsimony towards Central Asia, born of its deteriorating public finances, means that aid has hitherto been confined to a grant to Tajikistan of $50 million and $50 million in credits to Turkmenistan.[27] Indeed, Tehran has had to work hard to discourage the Tajiks, with whom the Persians are closest culturally, from expecting large amounts of aid.[28] This unpromising context appears to be confirmed by the experience of Iranian companies on the ground. They have been regarded with suspicion and even antipathy in much of Central Asia, notably Uzbekistan, for political and cultural reasons. Moreover, Iranian trade and financial institutions, such as Saderat Bank which has an office in Ashkhabad, have shared the widespread frustrations caused by local ignorance of trade and banking practice.[29]

Iran's location and its potential importance as a line of supply and communications has, however, helped it to develop some economic relations with Central Asia. Turkmenistan, owing to its adjacent location, provides the greatest potential. In May 1992 President Hashemi Rafsanjani inaugurated work on a rail link between the two countries from Mashhad to Sarakhs. A bus link between Mashhad and Ashkhabad and a weekly flight between the two countries was also introduced.[30] Iran views the provision of this infrastructure as important in developing links with other republics. It is hoped that Uzbekistan and, perhaps more speculatively, Kazakhstan will find such routes attractive.[31] Iran has in any case formally demonstrated its commitment to the development of a southern line of supply and communications by announcing that it would improve its own longitudinal rail network, and expand the Persian Gulf port of Bandar Abbas.[32] Tehran hopes that eventually it may also benefit from the routing of oil and gas pipelines from Central Asia, either directly to the Gulf or via Iranian territory to Turkey and on to Europe.

In the absence of territorial contiguity, *Turkey* has placed considerable emphasis on the establishment of infrastructure and communications which do not rely on terrestrial links. Airline flights with the Central Asian republics were, for example, established well in advance of Iran. But Turkey has devoted its greatest efforts to telecommunications, which have been described as the 'industrial frontiersman' of its Central Asian policy.[33] PTT, the public sector telecommunications company in Turkey, provided public telephone exchanges for the five republics free of charge, the aim being to tie Central Asia into the Turkish system. Ankara met with rather more mixed success in its attempts to provide Turkish television transmissions to the new republics. The governments of the new republics have been loath to forfeit their control over broadcasting, and have been reluctant to re-broadcast locally the transmissions from Turkey for mass consumption. The newly established channel for this purpose, Avrasia, has in any case proved to be rather dull and has hence made somewhat unattractive viewing.

In order to encourage the private sector to deal with Central Asia, the government of Turkey has proved to be supportive of the new states. Ankara extended credits worth $610 million to the Central Asian republics, with a further $340 million being forthcoming in the form of indirect loans, all to be administered through Turkey's Eximbank. Turkish companies have in turn responded, although their involvement has varied according to local circumstances.[34] Where local conditions are deemed to be right, especially regarding the prospects for political stability, such as in Turkmenistan, a significant Turkish involvement has been achieved. Thus there are currently 40 Turkish companies operating in Turkmenistan, and Turkish firms have signed nearly 70 per cent of all contracts between the Turkmen Ministry of Agriculture and Western companies.[35]

Conclusion

When the states of the former Soviet Union emerged as independent entities there was a widespread expectation that the Middle East would exercise considerable influence over them. This view quickly proved to be exaggerated. An over-preoccupation with Islam and the Turkic family of languages was a key reason behind this inflated expectation. In turn, the preoccupation with religion and language masked other characteristics shared by both regions, such as the nature of the respective state systems and political culture. The nature of politics, and for that matter macroeconomics, in Central Asia and the Middle East are indeed very similar.

Such similarities should not, however, be mistaken for evidence of a profound impact of one region upon the other. The relationship between them is actually very new. This political culture has evolved in parallel rather than by adoption. Geopolitics restricts the potential for the development of a strong interregional relationship, leaving Iran with a physical advantage over the other states of the Middle East. It will therefore be some time before the relationship between the Middle East and Central Asia acquires real ballast. Other states and regions are in any case at least as well placed as the Middle East to exert a gravitational pull upon the new Central Asia.

Interaction between the two regions is proceeding, but in a geographically and functionally patchy way. Israel, Turkey and Iran are at the forefront of such new ties, engaged in a strategy which might be described as neo-peripheralism. Of the Arab world, Saudi Arabia and to a lesser extent the rest of the Gulf Cooperation Council states have shown some interest in Central Asia. Formal ties have now been largely established. Political, economic and ideological links are in the process of being forged. The depth of the involvement of the two regions will determine the extent to which the states of one region become drawn into the politics of the other.

5

CENTRAL ASIA'S RELATIONS WITH AFGHANISTAN AND SOUTH ASIA

Anthony Hyman

Historical links between Central and South Asia (India and Pakistan) were close and important until the mid-nineteenth century, when the khanates of Turkestan came under Russian influence and rule. Since the break-up of the Soviet Union, changes in the political map make it quite natural to speculate whether, or how far, old patterns of relations will be restored.

Independence brought the formal setting-up of foreign embassies in Central Asian capitals, along with the rapid expansion of communications between the two regions, as well as with the Middle East and Western Europe. Geopolitical considerations include future access for the land-locked Central Asian republics through Afghanistan to a Pakistani port on the Indian Ocean, so as to supplement the present reliance on land routes to Black Sea ports.

However, Central Asian leaders have been at pains to emphasize that the development of economic and cultural relations with Pakistan, India, Afghanistan, Turkey or Iran would not be at the expense of their long-standing relations with Russia or other republics of the former Soviet Union. President Islam Karimov of Uzbekistan, for example, was typical of other Central Asian figures in stating, in October 1991:

> We see our future not in isolating ourselves from the republics surrounding us – especially fraternal ones – and from the entire Union. On the contrary, we see our future only in having as many ties as possible.

In a further interview he declared: 'I think it is obvious that we cannot suddenly break those ties that have been built over a number of decades.'[1]

Afghanistan

Compared with India and Pakistan, Afghanistan undoubtedly has the closest cultural and ethnic affinities with Central Asia. The main peoples of northern Afghanistan are essentially of the same ethnic stock as the Soviet 'nationalities' giving their names to the three Central Asian republics to the north of the Amu Darya: Uzbekistan, Tajikistan and Turkmenistan. Indeed, at least 500,000 Uzbeks, Tajiks and Turkmen of Afghanistan, besides a small number of Kyrgyz and Kazakhs, are descended from families of refugees who came from Fergana and other regions of Soviet Central Asia to Afghanistan only in the 1920s and 1930s, after the turmoil of the Russian revolution, civil war and forced collectivization. Most importantly, nearly twice as many Tajiks reportedly live in Afghanistan as in Tajikistan itself.

Like India, Afghanistan had maintained a consulate in Tashkent even before the declarations of independence. It was formally upgraded to an embassy at the end of 1991, but the political crisis inside Afghanistan remained too intense, and the 'government' in Kabul far too weak, to permit much attention to further developing relations with the republics. However, cooperation with the Central Asian republics in many varied fields is growing, and already trading links are considerable.

Much of this business is being transacted by private Afghan entrepreneurs based in Kabul and Mazar-i Sharif. Trading at the state level remains important, however, with petrol, for example, being imported from Turkmenistan, which has offered future technical help in exploiting Afghanistan's own gas and oil resources.

Afghanistan has large natural gas deposits centred in the Shibarghan area, and oilfields discovered so far mainly in the Saripul-Shibarghan region, close to the borders with Turkmenistan and Uzbekistan. Exploitation of Afghanistan's gas and oil reserves was entirely under Soviet direction from 1963, when the first large gas discovery was made. In effect, the USSR maintained a tight monopoly of development aid throughout northern Afghanistan, its exclusive sphere of influence, with 97 per cent of gas produced being piped to the USSR. Afghanistan remained totally dependent upon imported oil and kerosene, in spite of significant oil strikes, because no oil refinery was built, and domestic oil resources were neglected.

In the past Afghanistan had to reckon with four powerful direct neighbours: Pakistan to the southeast, Iran on the western border, the Soviet Union along the northern borders, and China across the Pamirs. Now in place of the USSR (often described by the PDPA regime in

Kabul as Afghanistan's 'Great Northern Neighbour') it has to reckon with three bordering Central Asian republics.

Gradually from 1978, and especially from 1980, after the Soviet military intervention, the PDPA government in Afghanistan came to rely upon Uzbekistan, Turkmenistan and Tajikistan as well as Russia itself to supply a range of goods in short supply. Political and economic links were rapidly expanded to bolster the Kabul regime, along with initiatives in higher education and culture. Thousands of Afghan students were sent to study at institutes or schools in Uzbekistan and Tajikistan. This was part of the 'internationalist duty' the Central Asian republics were obliged to perform as part of the Soviet strategy in Afghanistan.[2]

During the 1980s, Uzbekistan began to develop a variety of direct links with the northern provinces of Afghanistan, where ethnic Uzbeks are one of the dominant peoples. Independence for the republics to the north has served to increase the pressures from northern Afghanistan's major nationalities for greater autonomy from Kabul. The reality of irredentism as a potential force in the wider region cannot be ignored.

In the Soviet era, development projects funded by the USSR were almost all concentrated in the north of the country. Trade agreements concluded directly between the northern provinces of Afghanistan and the republics were often made on a bilateral basis, bypassing the central government in Kabul. Concentration on building roads, a railway, a river port and new bridges across the Amu Darya was part of an infrastructural network bringing closer together the northern regions of Afghanistan and Central Asia.

These new links were often interpreted in geopolitical terms as a Soviet political strategy to realign and integrate the economy of northern Afghanistan into that of the Central Asian republics. To a large extent, this process did take place. Historians, however, might be equally tempted to see in these developments the re-emergence of age-old trading links and political ties between Balkh, Herat and other regions of Afghanistan with the rest of Central Asia. These patterns had been interrupted and distorted from the late nineteenth century by Afghanistan's emergence as a buffer state between the Russian and British empires in Asia, together with a deliberate policy on the part of the Afghan and Soviet regimes of insulating their respective populations from cross-border contacts and influences.

Neighbouring and regional states already exert considerable influence over the political struggle inside Afghanistan, in its present condition a broken-backed state with a greatly weakened centre. Given the prospect of continuing political instability and, in many areas, the likelihood that 'warlords' in the form of semi-independent commanders will remain able to contest for power with an enfeebled and unstable central government, any realistic assessment must deal with the possibility of a disintegration of the country into its main ethnic and tribal components.

In the worst-case scenario, Afghanistan – a fragile state even before the civil war began in 1978 – will simply unravel. Tensions between those same diverse ethnic elements that once attracted foreign ethnographers (making some describe Afghanistan as a 'museum of peoples', or as an empire rather than a kingdom) could well prove to be a catalyst for disintegration. If this does happen, what is likely to succeed it?

The half of the country north of the Hindu Kush is now more than ever distinct from and to a large extent independent of the Pushtun-dominated south as well as the Kabul government. This practical independence is a result of the steady process throughout the 1980s of Pushtuns being forced out from the northern lands where they had been settled in a deliberate state policy. Together with the Persian-speaking Hazaras in the central regions, it is the Tajiks, Uzbeks and Turkmen who now stand out as the masters in what used in the nineteenth century to be called 'Afghan Turkestan', by analogy with Russian and Chinese Turkestan.

Any disintegration of Afghanistan would present neighbouring states with opportunities for territorial gains and in some cases for satisfying latent irredentist ambitions. At the least it would encourage stronger Central Asian governments to spread their influence over regions across the state borders. With political independence and the opening-up of borders, it is not only bilateral state relations but also informal contacts that are being developed rapidly between these artificially divided or scattered peoples.

Cross-border contacts have flourished since 1992 between the Tajik communities, many of them Ismailis, of Badakhshan in northeastern Afghanistan and Tajikistan's own Badakhshan Autonomous Region, which declared its independence from Dushanbe in April 1992, only to renounce it before engaging in negotiations. The civil wars and changes of regime in Afghanistan and Tajikistan in 1992 combined to produce a flow of refugees from Tajikistan into Afghanistan (as well as to other Central Asian republics), and another wave of Afghan refugees, mainly from Kabul, who took refuge in Tashkent, Dushanbe and Moscow.

One of the stranger aspects of this refugee flow was the 'homecoming', or rather repatriation, to Kazakhstan in the summer of 1993 of 4,000 ethnic Kazakh refugees from Afghanistan and Iran. Originally a number of Kazakh families had fled to Afghanistan and Iran in the 1920s, as a result of the civil war and savage reprisals against rebels by the Red Army. But in the early l980s, over 2,000 ethnic Kazakhs had been forced by the war to leave their homes in Afghanistan and find refuge in Iran. The long overland journey of the Kazakhs to their place of origin was helped by coordination and funding from the UN High Commissioner for Refugees (UNHCR).

Formal foreign relations with Afghanistan were greatly complicated by the escalation of fighting in the capital, Kabul, from January 1994. The government as such had virtually collapsed, along with basic services, and not one foreign embassy was left functioning by the spring. This seemed all the more ironic considering that Kabul had been the most international capital of the Central Asian region ever since the 1920s, when Afghanistan joined the League of Nations as one of a handful of independent Asian states.

Uzbekistan, Turkmenistan, Iran, Pakistan and Russia maintained consulates in either Jalalabad, Herat or Mazar-i-Sharif. The bilateral relations of northern Afghan provinces with the neighbouring republics of Central Asia were based more on contacts and patronage of individual leaders or warlords like Ismail Khan of Herat and General Abdul Rashid Dostum of Mazar than on links with a so-called 'government' in Kabul.

Just as much as Afghanistan, Tajikistan itself represented a threat to regional stability. The widening conflict, and the presence of a Russian-led CIS military force along the Tajikistan border with Afghanistan and at various locations in the republic, combined to create a potential international conflict there. Some degree of interaction has taken place between the two civil wars, with weapons from Afghanistan being made available to Tajik opposition activists, and training camps set up in Afghan territory close to the border. Commanders of rival Afghan parties were actively aiding Tajik opposition forces, albeit on a small scale.

However, the issue of foreign intervention was deliberately exaggerated and used by the Tajikistan regime – and initially by Russia as well – to confuse the central issue that a merciless civil war was being carried on between rival Tajik clans and parties. There was certainly no proof for the claims repeatedly made from Dushanbe and Tashkent that the Kabul government itself was directly involved in aiding the Tajik rebels.

The brutal repression of opposition sympathizers and rival clans in Tajikistan, which shares a 1,200 km border with Afghanistan, brought scores of thousands of desperate Tajik refugees across the Pianj river in the winter of 1992–3, seeking refuge in areas west of Kunduz. The fighting also led to frequent and sometimes fatal border clashes between

Russian army units and Tajik rebels. They provoked a retaliation by Russian troops in the form of artillery shelling of Afghan villages, which suffered hundreds of civilian casualties.

Fears were expressed by Russian critics in Moscow that the actions of Russian forces based along the Tajikistan border might well lead to another costly and unwanted Afghan war. Visits by ministers of the Afghanistan government to Dushanbe and Tashkent during the first part of 1993, including that of Burhanuddin Rabbani during his term as president, were intended to resolve these differences, but failed to do so.

The appeal of irredentist ideas has become manifest in unofficial nationalist circles at least, among Tajiks and Uzbeks. Ahmed Shah Massoud, a key minister in the Kabul government and an ethnic Tajik from Panjshir, made a series of statements about the possible future 'unification' of Tajiks living in Afghanistan and the republic of Tajikistan. These statements should probably not be taken at face value, since according to another interpretation they are meant more to put pressure on Massoud's political rivals and to strengthen the position of his alliance in northern Afghanistan.[3]

The so-called 'Uzbek militia' under General Dostum has grown greatly in size since the change of regime in Kabul in April 1992. At present it almost certainly constitutes the best-equipped trained military force in the country. General Dostum's forces and his *Junbish* ('national Islamic movement') will surely remain a power to reckon with. This movement's close links with the Karimov government, and valuable regular supplies it receives from across Uzbekistan's borders, indicate that Dostum's forces are seen as an important factor for future stability by this key neighbour, as well as by other regional states.

In the current greatly enfeebled state of Afghanistan, any 'government' is likely to be so weak as to be little more than a passive spectator rather than an actor in the redesigning and expansion of regional cooperation. However, Pakistan, if not other regional states, can be relied upon to back the principle of territorial integrity. For Pakistan, any *de facto* dismemberment of Afghanistan, or secession of the northern half of the country, would inevitably present a serious challenge to its own stability, because the mainly Pushtun tribal population of the southern half of Afghanistan is closely related to the Pushtuns (Pathans) of two Pakistani provinces – North West Frontier and Baluchistan.

In such an eventuality, many observers would expect a revival of the 'Pukhtunistan' ideal of a merger of the Pushtun lands, or of the call for independence for the Pushtuns of Pakistan. Though politically quiescent

since the 1970s (and even judged dead by some analysts), the Pukhtunistan issue constitutes 'a "permanent" irredentist cause at the disposal of
radical leaderships in both countries', and a latent source of conflict
between the two countries.[4]

Merely putting forward future political scenarios does not, of course,
bring them into being. The essence of the matter is that great uncertainty
prevails about the future of Afghanistan, and that internal power rearrange-
ments within Afghanistan – or in Tajikistan, for that matter – are very
likely to produce a wider regional impact, by challenging the respective
state borders, confirmed by British–Russian imperial commissions in the
late nineteenth century.

For Pakistan, Afghanistan represents the vital land-bridge between
Central Asia and South Asia: continued anarchy inside Afghanistan
would prevent the regular functioning of land transport routes for trade.
Afghanistan figures large for Uzbekistan too, in part because it is the
only non-CIS state with which that country has a border (though Turkmenistan has Iran as a neighbour, and Tajikistan has China). The three
bordering republics of Uzbekistan, Tajikistan and Turkmenistan are bound
to have closer relations with Afghanistan than are either Kyrgyzstan or
Kazakhstan.

India

Indian interest in the Central Asian region comes from a mixture of
politico-strategic concerns and, perhaps to a lesser extent, perceived
commercial prospects. For some political circles in India the independence of the ex-Soviet republics was interpreted in an alarmist fashion, as
a highly unwelcome strengthening of Pakistan's regional position, with
five potential new allies. The fact that Kazakhstan had stockpiles of
nuclear weapons and missiles on its territory, if not under its direct
control, inevitably increased India's concern to establish close relations.

There was fervid speculation in Indian nationalist circles, reflected in
the Indian media, that the shared religion of Islam would soon produce a
Muslim fundamentalist reaction and a close alliance between Pakistan
and the Central Asian republics. This line of reasoning was also encouraged, of course, by parallel predictions by the Western media. US Sena-
tor Pressler, on a visit to India in 1991, actually warned about the dangers
of a 'fundamentalist belt' of Muslim nations emerging in Central Asia.

However, India's government took a more sanguine view, that none of
the republics wanted the Islamic factor to count in their foreign relations,

and that India quite as much as Pakistan could keep or gain further influence with these essentially secular-minded governments. An important aspect of India's strategy has been the pursuit of its foreign policy interests, in particular putting across its case over the Kashmir issue. India was naturally keen to counter any progress by Pakistan.

India's favoured position in Central Asia arose from the special relationship it had enjoyed for decades with the Soviet Union. Indian culture had high prestige among the regional states, and there was considerable goodwill for the country and its people. The key to India's prestige in Central Asia, as in Russia itself, comes from neither politics, fine arts nor historical links, but instead from mass culture, in the form of the immensely popular Hindi film industry centred on Bombay, and the pop songs it spawns.

India's enormous influence upon the developing modern film industry of Central Asia is obvious. Even today, the image of Indian cinema and film stars is a glamorous one, like that of Hollywood throughout the Western world in earlier generations. Indian films still take up many of the columns in film magazines published in the Central Asian republics. What then is the great attraction of escapist Indian films in Soviet Central Asia – as in Russia?

The Central Asian film director Ali Khamraev explains it thus:

> You have to put yourself in the place of an average filmgoer who works hard all day in the fields, in the factory. And in the evening, you offer him a film about the problems of a communist workers' brigade! But in these Indian melodramas, he can lose himself, there is music, dancing, love, beautiful cars ... he wants to relax, to cry. And this is not the sign of primitivism. At bottom, our cultures are very close.[5]

Although these ties were cemented by the Friendship Treaty with the USSR in 1971, India has enjoyed close political links with the region for decades, and still retains much of its prestige as an old and trusted friend from the Soviet era. It is seen as a leading secular state of Asia, and a model for progress along the path of modernization and secularism favoured by the regimes in power in Central Asia. India was in a good position to exploit the changed conditions brought about by the disintegration of the USSR, because it already had a large consulate functioning in Tashkent, unlike most of the regional states.

As First Secretary of the Communist Party of Uzbekistan, Karimov made an official visit to India in August 1991. Arriving with a high-level delegation, he was flattered by the attentions paid him, for he was equated with the Vice-President of India and held discussions with the Prime Minister in New Delhi. Meetings with Indian business groups were only exploratory, but an Indian trade exhibition opened in Tashkent the very next month, intended to show off Indian machinery and electronic equipment.

Within days of Uzbekistan's declaration of independence in September 1991, India's existing consulate in Tashkent was upgraded to an embassy. It was under the able management of the consul and acting chargé, Ashok Mukherjee, an Indian diplomat with years of experience in the region. New Delhi attached definite importance to the region, and stringent Indian budget constraints on expansion of the foreign service were solved by retrenchment in Africa and other parts of the world, enabling India to open new embassies of considerable size in each of the Central Asian capitals (except Tajikistan, owing to political instability) early in 1992. India has actively promoted cooperation with all five Central Asian republics, inviting all their leaders to New Delhi and sending high-level Indian delegations to the capitals of the region.

To date, the actual volume of Indian trade with Central Asia has remained modest, but in markets and stores of the capitals, Indian soap, toiletries and other products are increasingly on sale. Uzbekistan is the main focus of interest. In January 1992, Uzbekistan and India signed a trade agreement for 1992 worth $75 million. Many other business opportunities were being examined, and the Indian firm Shaw Wallace reported at the end of the year a contract to set up a distillery in Uzbekistan and to supply Indian-produced liquor. As far as private trading was concerned, Indian exporters claimed that they faced higher freight charges compared with rivals situated closer to the region, because access to land-locked Central Asia was only through the Black Sea port of Odessa.

The size of the Indian community was estimated in 1992 at some 3,000 in Uzbekistan, made up mainly of students, many of them studying at Tashkent University or in institutes, and businessmen or representatives of Indian firms trading in the region. A third category came from Indian technicians and workers for Tata and other Indian companies who were constructing three big luxury hotel projects in Tashkent, Bukhara and Samarkand. Although the Indian component of these projects was virtually complete by autumn 1992, the opening of the hotels was seriously delayed by the failure of the Uzbek contractors to supply promised materials, including marble, and also by uncertainty over management contracts and responsibility for payment.

At the official level, India still benefited from the prestige it had enjoyed before the break-up of the Soviet Union. Thus on 15 August 1991 a public meeting was held in Tashkent to celebrate India's national independence day. A special programme marked a 'Soviet–Indian friendship week' which was devoted to the themes of India's independence and the twentieth anniversary of the Soviet–Indian Treaty of Peace, Friendship and Cooperation. This week was inaugurated in Tashkent with a show in a 'House of Culture' named after Indira Gandhi, at which singers and dancers clad in national costumes of the various states of India performed. A similar event took place one year later, with a festival of Indian films and other shows in cities of Uzbekistan, and a series of annual celebrations was planned.

The Indian Prime Minister Narasimha Rao made a regional tour in May 1993. With Uzbekistan a Treaty 'On the Principles of Inter-State Relations' was signed, a version of the old Soviet Treaty of Peace, Friendship and Cooperation, with the exception that no reference was made to military cooperation. Further claims made as to the unanimity of views and policies of the two countries seemed distinctly overblown. Both governments had jointly pledged to combat 'state-sponsored terrorism' and had shown 'remarkable commonality' in their will to combat regional terrorism, arms- and drug-trafficking and 'extremist ideologies'. However, neither Rao nor Karimov identified which countries they were referring to. Most observers presumed that India meant Pakistan's sponsorship of 'terrorism' in Kashmir, while Uzbekistan meant involvement in the civil war in Tajikistan, whether by Afghanistan, Pakistan or other foreign states.

New air and trading links between the two countries were agreed, and India offered a credit of US$10 million to Uzbekistan. India proposed the opening of a cultural centre in Tashkent as well as the provision of technical equipment to receive Indian TV programmes for 90 minutes daily in Tashkent. At the same time, the existing student exchange programme between the two countries was expanded.

In Almaty Mr Rao and his team met government representatives, and were offered participation in the space programmes and technological development at the Baikonur cosmodrome. India extended a $10 million credit to Kazakhstan, the same amount as in the previous year. Credits of only half this amount were offered to Turkmenistan and Kyrgyzstan.

Abdul Malik Abdullajanov, the Prime Minister of Tajikistan, finally visited India in February 1993; he was the last leader from a Central Asian state to do so. India offered a $5 million trade credit and six agreements aimed at increasing bilateral trade as well as cultural, banking, technical and sporting links. In spite of the political crisis in Tajikistan – which had prevented India progressing with its plan to start up an embassy in Dushanbe – Indian private companies were reportedly looking closely at Tajikistan's investment potential in silver, pharmaceuticals, coal, granite and leather goods for joint ventures.

India's Minister for Foreign Affairs, Salman Khursheed, made a tour of the Central Asian republics in June 1994, accompanied by a group of Indian businessmen. In Kazakhstan, where Khursheed spent three days, he was bluntly told by President Nazarbayev that 'much more' could be done for trade promotion and investment. But some of the planned joint ventures had come into operation, including in the capital, Almaty, an Indian cultural centre and restaurant, as well as a Kazakh–Indian business council. Regular flights between Almaty and Delhi started in July. Besides Indian plans with the big three republics, Khursheed discussed a variety of new joint ventures in Kyrgyzstan and pledged a $5 million loan to Tajikistan, part of a cooperation programme intended to promote joint projects in industry.

However, the civil war in Tajikistan inevitably eroded foreign confidence in the viability of business ventures, and kept away Indian as well as other foreign business visitors. Dangers to life and property were not by any means restricted to Tajik nationals, with reported robberies and murders of Pakistani and other foreign visitors to Dushanbe from mid-1992.

The rapid growth in Pakistan's presence in Central Asia from 1991 met with concern and keen resentment in Indian nationalist circles. It was even assumed that Pakistan, together with Iran and Turkey, would manage to create a Muslim bloc of states in Central Asia, and the prospect of Muslim fundamentalism spreading across Central Asia was raised. These fears may have helped produce what looks like a misinformation campaign mounted in the form of a number of sensational reports broadcast by All-India radio.

It was claimed, for example, in January 1992 that Pakistan had already gained from this new relationship by purchasing stocks of enriched uranium from Tajikistan for its nuclear programme. India, for its part, had failed to respond to an offer by Kyrgyzstan to sell enriched uranium to India under International Atomic Energy Agency safeguards. Further Indian reports maintained, without solid evidence, that Kazakhstan was planning to supply Pakistan with nuclear weapons from the large stocks in the republic in the control of Russian armed forces.

Any balanced analysis of India's policy towards the Central Asian republics would have to keep in mind that from New Delhi's perspective, its long-standing partner Russia remained of overwhelming importance for arms supplies, trade in general and technical and scientific cooperation. But New Delhi showed determination to stay in the front rank of Asian states in building relations with the independent republics.

Pakistan

Pakistan has showed great keenness in exploiting new openings in Central Asia. Geopolitical ambitions merged here with Islamic ideology and commercial acumen to produce a dynamic policy. Even if Pakistan's Central Asian initiatives came from a combination of largely pragmatic motives, their deliberate interpretation as pan-Islamic policies certainly improved the self-image of the Nawaz Sharif administration. And Pakistan's natural interests in the region ensured that it remained a significant priority for the subsequent government of Benazir Bhutto.

In taking a series of initiatives in Central Asia, Pakistan's government was acting in the public arena and at the same time playing to its own domestic public, where Islamist influence was considerable. For the Jamiat-i-Islami and other small Islamic-oriented parties in the government coalition, Pakistan's swift reorientation towards Central Asia was judged, indeed, one of the most positive aspects of its performance.

The springboard for launching initiatives in Central Asia was clearly the break-up of the USSR, with the relaxation of tight controls exercised by Moscow over the republics' foreign links. Pakistan's international relations had grown remarkably through the previous decade, helped by the Soviet invasion of Afghanistan together with adroit handling by General Zia-ul-Haq. Pakistan developed close links with the USA, Iran and many states of the Middle East, particularly in the Gulf, while at the same time attracting large aid and investment from Western Europe, Japan and international financial institutions. These various successes enhanced the importance of foreign policy for Pakistan.[6]

Yet, as Robert Wirsing shrewdly wrote, 'it has been Pakistan's distinct misfortune to have needed foreign allies far more than they have ever needed Pakistan.'[7] It is, indeed, a great misfortune for Pakistan that its main rival and regional adversary is India, which by its sheer size and economic weight must usually be reckoned a more appealing strategic alternative for foreign powers. This long-standing rivalry with India to a great extent explains Pakistan's eagerness to develop relations with

Central Asia. Glib arguments about Pakistan achieving vital 'strategic depth' in Central Asia against India in the event of a future fourth war were often heard in Islamabad.

Another aspect of growing regional links is religion. Visits by religious figures to and from Pakistan, as well as donations made by Pakistani-based Islamic organizations like Jamiat-i-Islami for building mosques and promoting religious education in Central Asia, were meant to further the goal of Islamic brotherhood. This process had actually begun before independence. A group of influential imams of mosques in Tajikistan, for example, had been invited in 1989, visiting the international headquarters of the Motamar (the Saudi-funded 'World Muslim Congress') in Karachi.

Mufti Sadikh, Chairman of the Muslim Board for Central Asia and Kazakhstan, visited Pakistan in 1990 and 1991, reaching an agreement (in July 1990) with Pakistan's Ministry of Religious Affairs for a donation of ten million rupees to help with mosque-building, Islamic literature and videos, a printing press and scholarships for Central Asian students of Islam. Religious issues also formed one of the topics of a series of public seminars and conferences held in Pakistani cities from 1990 based around the theme of ex-Soviet Central Asia opening up to the world.

Sufism, the mystical path of Islam, is another bond linking Central Asia with Pakistan, Turkey and other Muslim countries. The most influential Sufi 'tarika' (order) in Central Asia are the Nakshbandis, who are also prominent in South Asia. They stand relatively close to Muslim orthodoxy, unlike many of the smaller Sufi orders. Visits by foreign leaders or dignitaries from Muslim countries, often accompanied by gifts of money for the upkeep of the main Nakshbandi Sufi shrines of Central Asia, have become commonplace in recent years. There appears to be reciprocal interest. The visit of a Nakshbandi shaikh of Pakistan caused a stir in May 1992, with a large, enthusiastic crowd greeting him in Namangan, a religious-minded town in the Fergana Valley of Uzbekistan.

Overall Pakistan had very important economic interests in the region. Its economic priorities were clear: developing bilateral trade in raw materials and manufactured goods, opening up communications and contracting for regular power supplies. The initial goal was to start up direct air flights between the various capitals of Central Asia and Pakistan. A longer-term goal was a projected highway and railway across Afghanistan to Pakistan, giving trade access to the Indian Ocean. Pakistan saw substantial benefits for its industrial growth in obtaining regular supplies of surplus power, through gas and electricity grid schemes or through future oil supplies from Tajikistan, Turkmenistan, Kazakhstan and Uzbekistan.

Besides manufacturing and light industry, Pakistani entrepreneurs felt they had a great deal to offer in setting up or expanding banking and insurance as well as stock markets, joint-venture capital and import–exports, all sectors particularly poorly developed in Central Asia, and where training is badly needed. Here, however, Pakistani firms faced considerable competition from Turkey, India and other countries of Asia as well as from Europe and North America. Some goodwill for Pakistan, and interest in what it has to offer, may indeed exist, but there is also caution and a natural tendency in the Central Asian capitals to wait and see what other commercial offers are made.

The theme of economic cooperation between Pakistan and its Muslim neighbour states is hardly new. Speculation about the need for and potential benefits from an 'Islamic Common Market' dates back at least two decades. With five of the ex-Soviet Muslim republics as well as Afghanistan joining the ECO, it is only to be expected that some Islamic visionaries in Pakistan are reviving their hopes of achieving for the region what the European Community has achieved in Europe. They clearly aspire to lead Central Asia into a bright new world using Pakistani experience.[8]

However, any such ambitions of offering Pakistan as another role model to the Central Asian republics, like Turkey and Iran, are firmly rejected by Pakistan's diplomatic representatives in the region. They project more modest and more realistic expectations. 'Each country has its own pace, and the Central Asian republics certainly move slowly. It is only realistic to expect a slow but steady pace of development through ECO', maintained a Pakistani ambassador to a Central Asian capital, in an interview in September 1992.

In a first foray, a 26-strong Pakistani government delegation was sent in December 1991 to the Central Asian republics, paying short visits to each capital in turn. It was led by Sardar Asif Ali, Minister of State for Economic Affairs. A high Pakistani priority was the building up of relations with Uzbekistan, as the biggest potential market and arguably the key republic in political terms for the future. Indeed, Pakistan's expanding economic links with Central Asia, as well as some of the difficulties encountered, can be illustrated by the case of Uzbekistan.

Pakistan offered the country a revolving credit of $30 million for purchase of Pakistani engineering goods, and assured the newly independent republic of 'full diplomatic support' in its attempts to obtain membership of the UN and the Organization of Islamic Countries (OIC). The opening in Tashkent of a branch of the National Bank of Pakistan in 1992 was the first operation by any foreign bank in Uzbekistan.

In Pakistan's business circles, active pursuit of economic opportunities centred inevitably on Uzbekistan, helped by the start-up in 1992 of direct flights between Tashkent and Islamabad and Tashkent and Karachi by the two respective national airlines, PIA and Uzbekistan Hava Yollari (created out of Aeroflot in 1992). As well as Pakistani tourists, many businessmen from Punjab, Karachi and the North West Frontier came to see things for themselves and investigate commercial openings. Then in April 1994 PIA widened its existing network in Central Asia by inaugurating flights to Ashkhabad and Baku from Karachi. These flights were expected to promote bilateral trade and tourism.

Among the early visitors was the chairman of the 'Forum of the Restoration of the Pakistan Economy', Abdul Razzak Rajwani, who visited Tashkent, Dushanbe and Baku in December 1991 to explore markets for Pakistani exports of textiles, garments and foodstuffs. He claimed there was indeed a big potential market, but admitted the problem of currency exchange rates, which effectively meant that barter trading would be the only viable system.

Many of the joint ventures announced were small-scale, but some larger operations were also set up. Pakistan's Tabani Corporation was notably active in marketing pharmaceuticals and cotton, and in tourism and other service sectors. It obtained a profitable agency in Pakistan for sales of tickets for Uzbekistan Hava Yollari flights between Karachi and Tashkent, and in a goodwill gesture backed a number of events of cultural or sporting significance in Uzbekistan.

For Pakistani as for Indian businessmen, Central Asia's cotton sector is an obvious attraction, with prices of raw cotton remarkably low since the collapse of the rouble's value. As mentioned in Chapter 3, Turkmenistan, Tajikistan and Uzbekistan produced raw cotton for the whole of the Soviet Union, but nearly all the processing was done in Russia and Ukraine. Now there is a natural ambition to industrialize. Pakistan offered to help in increasing the capacity for textiles and cotton yarn production. Great potential is also said to exist for Pakistani firms wishing to export machinery for oil crushing and cotton ginning.

In Kazakhstan, there was an exchange of letters of intent to build a luxury hotel in Almaty and to set up a cellular telecommunications network. Pakistan's Tabani Group entered briskly into business with an agreement reportedly worth $50 million to export food and consumer goods to Kazakhstan, some from Pakistan. Training of Kazakh business managers in Pakistan was agreed with Almaty University.

A much lower degree of Pakistani activity took place in Turkmenistan and Kyrgyzstan, though trade credits were offered. It was in Tajikistan, the poorest of the five republics, that Pakistan made apparent progress, with a memorandum of understanding signed for mutual cooperation in many areas. Tajikistan's offer to supply Pakistan with hydroelectricity through a power line across Afghan territory would, however, have to wait on peace and stability in Afghanistan.

Meanwhile, a team of Pakistani economic and fiscal experts was invited to establish new management systems in the government. The Institute of Management and Policy in Lahore agreed to train Tajiks in business studies, while in the commercial field, textile and telephone deals were made with Pakistani companies, together with an agreement to build a luxury hotel in Dushanbe. Bilateral exchanges of youth delegations and students were also agreed.

Official visits between Pakistan and Central Asia mushroomed from early 1992. Nazarbayev paid a visit to Pakistan in February of that year; he signed a series of protocols for cooperation, with industrial deals and joint ventures proposed in Kazakhstan.

Pakistan's Prime Minister, Nawaz Sharif, himself made a formal tour of Central Asian capitals in June 1992. Uzbekistan was one of the main focuses of attention. In a letter to Karimov the previous year, Sharif had stressed 'the strong bonds of culture, history, religion and tradition that have existed between Pakistan and Uzbekistan'. Talks were held in Tashkent between Sharif and Karimov, but little real warmth or trust was generated. In a series of speeches and statements Karimov continued to claim that both Pakistan and Afghanistan were providing military instructors for training Tajik rebels fighting in Tajikistan against the regime backed by troops supplied by Russia and Uzbekistan.[9] This suspicion may have been a deciding factor in Karimov's decision not to offer Pakistan participation in development of new oil and gas reserves in Uzbekistan.

Pakistan had shown great interest in becoming involved in oil and gas production, but these hopes were dashed in February 1993, when a bilateral protocol for oil and gas development in Uzbekistan was signed instead with Ukraine. The Ukrainian premier Leonid Kuchma stated that Karimov himself had told him that the oil and gas protocol had been originally intended for Pakistan.

Pakistan had initially placed considerable hopes on cooperation with

Tajikistan, although the civil war which developed there from the second half of 1992 placed in doubt virtually every project. A Tajik delegation led by I. Daulatom, Minister for Finance and Economic Affairs, had visited Pakistan in April 1992, and signed a fixed-price contract to supply Pakistan from 1997 with 1,000 megawatt of electricity for a 30-year period, via Afghanistan. In return Pakistan would over five years provide goods to a value of $500 million, some of which would be utilized to complete a partly constructed 300-megawatt dam close to Dushanbe.

Tajikistan expressed interest in importing drugs and commissioning a cement plant, also requesting Pakistani banks to set up branches in Dushanbe. The government pledged that any Pakistani bank willing to establish itself in the republic would be allowed to buy up to 50 per cent of shares in Tajikistan's foreign trade bank, and also be invited to rename the street in which the bank was to be located after a Pakistani city. Meanwhile, Dushanbe was twinned with Lahore, and a 'Pakistan-Tajik friendship society' was started in 1992 – or rather revived, according to its spokesmen, after a lapse of 26 years.

Then, in May 1994, Pakistan signed an agreement with Turkmenistan to train a batch of new cadets for Turkmenistan's airforce. This development in a sensitive area of state policy was the first move to lessen the long-standing monopoly of Russia in providing military training.

By mid-1994 there were some obvious setbacks to Pakistan's early ambitions of rapidly becoming a major player in regional trade and relations. Improving land communications to and from Central Asia depended upon peace and stability in Afghanistan, but with fighting raging in Kabul and some other regions of Afghanistan, construction of a railway and upgrading the existing highway proved impossible. Moreover, the scale of participation by Pakistani private business firms in the Central Asian region was disappointing, with numerous projected schemes languishing for lack of funding.

However, Pakistan, like Russia and Uzbekistan, tried to play a constructive role in resolving the civil war in Tajikistan. It offered to host a peace conference in Islamabad, after a first round of talks held in Moscow in April between Tajik opposition leaders and the regime controlling Dushanbe.

The Economic Cooperation Organization
The ECO was originally established as the economic (specifically development-oriented) counterpart of the Central Treaty Organization (CENTO),

the military grouping of conservative, pro-Western Middle Eastern states. Ten countries are now linked in ECO; it was enlarged in 1992 by the three original members Iran, Turkey and Pakistan to take in the five Central Asian republics, the Transcaucasian republic of Azerbaijan as well as Afghanistan. With a total population of almost three hundred million, and covering a vast area, the ECO countries have considerable economic potential which could be better exploited by closer coopera-tion. The sheer size of this grouping alone was enough to generate hopes and fantasies in some circles.

Each of the ten countries linked were Muslim, or had large Muslim populations. Was this the first stage towards creating an 'Islamic Com-mon Market'? Is ECO a contemporary pan-Islamic initiative – or instead a purely commercial and economic bloc of regional states? Such ques-tions are natural; but the answers depend very much on the ideological perspective of the enquirer. Official circles in Iran and Turkey are poles apart on this, while Pakistan stands somewhere in between. As for the secular-minded governments of the Central Asian republics, none of them desired their shared Muslim religion to intrude as a factor in their relations with neighbours.

In spite of official denials, it became clear that a contest for influence was going on between Iran, Turkey and Pakistan. Pakistani spokesmen disagreed strongly with the Turks, who emphasized that this was a secular initiative with political rather than religious significance for the future.

Pakistan's Foreign Minister, M. Siddiq Khan Kanju, typified the emotional or frankly romantic approach to Central Asia commonly seen in Pakistan when he declared, at the inaugural ceremony of the ECO Cultural Association in Islamabad in November 1992: 'It is like long-lost brothers meeting once again and joining in a deep embrace.' Kanju declared that ECO was actually incomplete without the Central Asian states. He chose to emphasize their common links: 'Central Asia has been the main home of all our people and by joining with them we are reaching back to the original homeland of many amongst us.'[10]

In the long term, the development of trade and joint ventures between Pakistan and Central Asia will also need massive investment in infra-structure and close cooperation with Afghanistan for the construction of new or improved roads as well as railway and pipeline links. From its own resources, Pakistan's government cannot afford the necessary in-vestment any more than can the other ECO states. What is certainly feasible, though, is progress through coordinated economic schemes, with the republics in partnership with Pakistani banks and large companies, as well as drawing upon international capital.

In opening up communications, Iran, Turkey and Pakistan, as well as China and India, are all active. Pakistan was one of the main contenders in improving and extending Central Asia's telephone communications with the outside world.

The Investment Development Bank for ECO, intended to fund joint projects in Central Asia, has total funds of close on $400 million, but clearly cannot make much of an impact on an area that is so large and that has such big problems. There is an obvious disparity between the boundless ambitions of the leading states in ECO and practical limitations of both finance and technology.

It is surely significant that bilateral relations between Pakistan and the various republics continued to be more important than those promoted within the framework of ECO. Cultural agreements were being prepared at the end of 1993, on the lines of those already in existence with China and Russia, between Pakistan's ministry for culture and those of the various Asian republics. They covered educational exchanges, television and visits by their respective troupes of dancers and musicians. The more rapid development of tourism on a state basis, as a part of wider cultural relations, was planned for the future.

There were signs by the end of 1992 that Pakistan, like Turkey, was beginning to benefit to a certain extent from international business interest in Central Asia. New investment of $100 million in Pakistan announced by the International Finance Corporation (IFC) of Washington DC was combined in 1992 with the upgrading of the IFC office in Islamabad to become a fully-fledged regional mission to cover the Central Asian republics and Afghanistan as well as Pakistan.[11]

Conclusion

Pakistan's bilateral links with the various states in Central Asia, based on a shared religion and common economic interests, are bound to grow further. But Pakistan made no headway with any of the Central Asian republics in its declared policy of isolating Israel, a policy that was in harmony with Iran, Saudi Arabia and most Muslim governments. As described in Chapter 4, Israel for its part vigorously promoted its relations with the various governments, and achieved substantial success based partly on help from the Jewish communities in or originally from Central Asia, but also on Israeli expertise in technology for agriculture in dry-water lands. The clear lesson for Pakistan, as for other Muslim states, was that the bond of Islam had strict limits: none of the Central Asian governments is prepared to restrict its foreign relations by following the ideological line of others on the Palestine issue.

For the coming decade, Pakistan intends to develop tourist links from their current low levels. Pakistani entrepreneurs estimate there is considerable scope for expansion of tourism to selected Central Asian destinations, given adequate investment in infrastructure and skilful management. The allure of the ancient Silk Roads, like the names of Tamerlane and Babur, founder of the Mongol empire, count for something in Pakistan as in India. Pakistani companies intending to undertake hotel construction and management showed a particular interest in Uzbekistan's great historic centres of Samarkand and Bukhara, besides Tashkent. For the future, tourist destinations in other republics, including mountain resorts, were being seriously considered.

The precise shape of bilateral relations for the 1990s remained uncertain. It is natural to ask about Central Asia, as Peter Lyon has done in the case of South Asia, whether the region will become 'a strategic cul-de-sac or a major cross-roads in the world's circulatory system of weapons, transport and trade in the 1990s'.[12]

Nevertheless, regardless of whether or how far the Central Asian republics manage to break free from Russian influence and economic power, Pakistan, India and Afghanistan will be keen to develop and strengthen their relations with the countries of this region – one which was arguably peripheral to Russia for the past century, as well as closed off to outside influences. The diverse contacts opening up with South Asia will surely help in the transition process of making Central Asia's formal independence into something more substantial.

6
THE NEW CENTRAL ASIA AND CHINA

Peter Ferdinand

The historical legacy

Present-day Xinjiang occupies one-sixth of the total area of the People's Republic of China (PRC) – 530,000 sq. km. It is larger than Uzbekistan and Turkmenistan, and second only to Kazakhstan in size, but its population of over 15 million is smaller than that of Kazakhstan and Uzbekistan, and represents only 1.2 per cent of the total population of China. Like the states of former Soviet Central Asia, its territory is as varied as it is enormous. As a consequence, geography has both caused and reinforced the evolution of different life-styles of its ethnic communities. The main divide has been between the wandering pastoral nomads of the north, predominantly Kazakhs, and the more settled inhabitants of the oases, who are mainly Uighurs.

Over the centuries the peoples of Xinjiang defined their identities in contradistinction to other groups, both neighbours and 'outsiders'. The concept of the most numerous local nationality, the Uighur, for example, gradually developed to distinguish major groups of indigenous Turkic-speakers from outsiders, most notably the Han Chinese,* and the various forms of political organization which they attempted to impose upon the region.[1] Yet, as was remarked in Chapter 2, the majority of the local inhabitants, right up to the twentieth century, owed primary loyalties to kinship groups and tribes associated with particular localities, especially oases, rather than to some larger ethnic community.

Historically, Xinjiang is part of the enormous area to the north and west of the core areas of China which was a constant source of anxiety to

---

* The term Han Chinese is used to denote the ethnic Chinese in the region.

Chinese emperors, because of the danger that a hostile army might suddenly materialize from there and overwhelm them. Xinjiang was seen as the door to Mongolia, and Mongolia was seen (at least in more recent centuries) as the door to the capital in Beijing. The potential threat from the region was regarded in the same way by the Tsars after centuries of occupation of Russia by the Mongol hordes. Thus the fear of resurgent Mongol armies led both Russia and China to attempt to control the region, but this also sometimes provoked rivalry and clashes between them.

For China such control was difficult, expensive and subject to enormous fluctuations. According to Owen Lattimore, writing in the 1930s, the Chinese had effectively controlled Central Asia for only 425 out of 2,000 years.[2] In 1760 China appeared at the height of its power, with much of Central Asia isolated and dependent upon it. Within a century the Qing system there had crumbled, as the result of growing Russian influence and native Muslim-based rebellions. The most serious such rebellion took place in the 1860s in the Ili region. It was led by Yaqub Beg, who set up an East Turkestan government, and was only suppressed in 1878. Millions of people died either in the fighting or as a result of famine and disease.

In 1884 Xinjiang was formally incorporated into the Chinese empire. In the first half of the twentieth century, however, its relationship with the rest of China was weak. There were several armed uprisings. From the collapse of the Qing empire in 1911, peace in the region alternated with fighting of intense savagery.[3] Between 1937 and 1942 it was ruled by a warlord, Sheng Shicai, with Soviet support. The establishment of the Soviet Union, and Soviet control over former Russian Central Asia, created an alternative pole of attraction for local leaders, especially at a time when central control of China was evaporating under the pressure of warlords. Links with the Soviet Union offered a geopolitical alternative to dependence upon China, and in addition the recently constructed Turkmenistan–Siberian railway provided a connection with the outside world which was much more convenient than having to pass through a China ravaged by civil war, warlords and the Japanese. The Soviet Union also offered economic aid. It was thanks to Soviet assistance that oil exploration began in Xinjiang. The Soviet regime was interested in Xinjiang as a border region, and because of fears of a Japanese invasion. Once again the interests of the peoples of Xinjiang were subordinated to the interests of great-power politics. An 'independent' Kazakh and Uighur East Turkestan Republic was established with Soviet support in 1933, then suppressed, only to be re-established in 1944. It controlled the northwestern Ili region until 1946.

Towards the end of the Chinese civil war Xinjiang was captured by forces of the People's Liberation Army (PLA) under the command of General Wang Zhen, and he and the first Party Secretary, Wang Enmao, were to rule over it for most of the following forty years.

Xinjiang and regional security

China's security

After 1949 one of the most immediate concerns of the leaders of the People's Republic was to restore unified control over the whole of China. In many ways Xinjiang typified their general preoccupations. Russian proximity to, and occasionally interference in, Xinjiang, was of continuing concern to Beijing from 1949 until the late 1980s. At the time of Liberation, many people in Xinjiang still thought of Soviet control as preferable to Chinese, especially as the standard of living on the Soviet side of the border was higher. It took the PRC a few years to stabilize its control, and Chinese currency did not begin to replace local and Soviet currencies in the province as a whole until November 1951.[4]

The population of Xinjiang at the time of Liberation was dominated by local minorities, chiefly Uighur and Kazakh. Only eight per cent of the population at that time were Han Chinese. In the 1950s Uighur elites suffered serious repression to prevent them from posing another secessionist threat. Then troubles between the Han Chinese and minorities during the Great Leap Forward escalated into a major revolt in 1962 in Ining and Tacheng. After its suppression up to 70,000 people fled across the frontier into Kazakhstan. In the aftermath the PLA set about sealing the frontier with the Soviet Union, and cross-border trade was banned.

Since 1949 there has been a steady influx of Han Chinese into the region, and for the first three decades at least the state seems deliberately to have encouraged this. It is possible to distinguish several waves of new settlers. First there were the remnants of the Nationalist armies which surrendered there to the Red Army, and were forced to settle down to life in farming, industry or construction. Many PLA soldiers who found themselves in Xinjiang at the end of the civil war or their period of military service were demobilized there. Both former nationalist and former communist soldiers were organized into the Xinjiang Production and Construction Corps. In 1984 its staff and their families numbered two-and-a-quarter million people.[5] The corps has been run as an autonomous unit, and its members have reclaimed land, run state farms and built factories, highways and railways. They operate largely autonomously and produce about half of the region's cotton and a quarter of its grain, and account for about twenty per cent of local GNP.[6] The second wave consisted of skilled technical and administrative personnel who were drafted to the region, especially during the 1950s but in succeeding decades as well, to assist in its development. Thirdly there were the young people drafted to the countryside of distant provinces after the end of the Cultural Revolution. In the fourth wave were former inmates of prison camps in Central Asia who stayed on after release, mainly because (at least until the later 1980s) they could be prevented from returning to their homes further east. Lastly there are people attracted by the opportunities offered by the economic reforms of the 1980s, whether as a result of the abolition of commune-based farming, or the toleration of private urban companies.

The end result of all these developments is that by the early 1990s the number of Han Chinese in Xinjiang had risen to 5.7 million, or 37.6 per cent of the total population of 15.2 million. Nevertheless the Uighur are still the largest community, with 7.19 million (47.5 per cent). Kazakhs comprise 1.12 million (7.3 per cent), and Kyrgyz and Mongols each almost 140,000 (0.9 per cent), whilst ethnic Chinese Muslims number 682,000 (4.5 per cent). Overall 60.1 per cent of the population consist of Muslim believers or of nationalities traditionally associated with Islam. [7]

During the Cultural Revolution large numbers of Red Guards were drafted into Xinjiang, and they set about undermining the identity of the ethnic minorities, destroying mosques and religious symbols, and forcing Muslims to eat pork, and minorities to speak only Chinese. In itself the presence of increasing numbers of Han Chinese in Xinjiang intensified frictions with the native population. Accusations of collusion between natives and people across the Soviet border were commonplace.

This relationship was aggravated by two further factors. The first has been the stationing of large numbers of PLA troops in the region to serve as a defensive line against attack from the Soviet Union. This has strengthened the colonial feel to the maintenance of law and order, especially as most of the PLA troops are Han Chinese. It is still largely the PLA, rather than the Armed Police, which is responsible for internal security in Xinjiang. The second factor has been the use of Xinjiang for the testing of atomic and nuclear weapons, which has had the effect of irradiating parts of the region.

In the 1980s the Chinese government attempted to involve more local people in administration and to make amends for earlier harsh treatment.

Efforts were made to rebuild mosques, to re-establish the freedom to practise the Muslim religion, and to use minority languages in local administration and education.

Yet this more conciliatory stance allowed long-standing grievances to be voiced more openly. For example, there were occasional public protests even in Beijing by students from Xinjiang, complaining about the nuclear test sites. However much the regime might proclaim its desire in the early 1980s to turn over a new leaf in its relations with the region, it was difficult for the local population to take this simply at face value. Disputes simmered. One experienced visitor to Xinjiang remarked in the mid-1980s on the frequent public fights between Chinese and Uighur youth and on the fear of the Uighur elites about absorption by the Chinese.[8]

All of these problems worried the leadership in Beijing and there were clear disagreements over how the issues should be handled. Some, such as then party General Secretary Hu Yaobang, were prepared for more conciliatory policies. He advocated more genuine consideration for local needs, and the phased withdrawal of Han Chinese officials. Others wanted to take a much tougher line. A hardline Han official was quoted as saying: 'You give them autonomy and they will only turn around and create an East Turkestan. Hu Yaobang also wants to withdraw Han cadres to the interior. That would be surrendering Xinjiang to the Soviet Union and Turkey. Only a traitor would do such a thing. To stabilize Xinjiang we must send hardliners like Wang Zhen.'[9]

Security relations with former Soviet Central Asia
Not only are Xinjiang's relations with the rest of China complex, so too are its relations with its neighbours in the FSU. First there is the simple length of the frontier. Xinjiang's borders with neighbouring states to the north and west stretch for 4,000 km. There have been significant disputes over various stretches. Then there is the legacy of frictions dating from the Great Leap Forward and the Cultural Revolution. More importantly, however, the quasi-independence which was forced upon the Central Asian republics has given rise to a new upsurge of nationalist feeling and new security concerns on both sides of the frontier. The grievances about Russian exploitation of the region can easily strike a chord with some of the minorities in Xinjiang, whilst the fact that Kazakhstan retains control of the nuclear weapons stationed on its soil worries the Chinese military high command.

Yet in general the situation is one which Beijing ought to be able to control. The population of Xinjiang is small and scattered. The Uighur are less numerous than the Uzbeks or the Kazakhs. All the ethnic groups are quite divided amongst themselves. The Uighur elites, at least in the 1980s, were described as being divided between those who live north of the Tianshan mountains, are more secular and might look to Soviet Central Asia or even China for stimulation and contact, and those in the Kashgar region to the west who focus more upon the predominantly Muslim culture.[10] These divisions might be manipulated again, as they have been in the past.

Moreover, the leaderships of the republics in FSU have no great interest in provoking confrontation with China – in fact rather the contrary. They have a great many worries of their own without wishing to antagonize such a populous neighbour. It is true that in Kazakhstan a non-violent Kazakh nationalist party is allowed to exist, and the chief plank of its programme is reunification with the Kazakh nation in Xinjiang. And in June 1992 a new political party calling for a Free Uighurstan was announced by leaders in Kyrgyzstan. Yet they cannot afford to provoke China. They are only too well aware of their weakness. Even the retention of nuclear weapons by Kazakhstan was undertaken with an eye to deterring possible Chinese incursions into the region.

In 1992 the Presidents of Kazakhstan, Uzbekistan, Turkmenistan and Kyrgyzstan all visited China, and in April 1994 Prime Minister Li Peng made a lengthy return visit. In his speeches he regularly affirmed China's interest in stability and security in the region.[11] A number of agreements were signed on various forms of cooperation. A 'historic' border agreement was signed with Kazakhstan, although not yet with Kyrgyzstan. President Karimov of Uzbekistan made comments which were interpreted as offering support for the Chinese attempts to contain Uighur separatism.[12] President Nazarbayev explicitly committed himself to preventing advocates of an 'East Turkestan Republic' from working against China and interfering in Xinjiang from the territory of Kazakhstan.[13]

Nevertheless the security situation from the Chinese point of view remains less than satisfactory. In April 1990 a group of Kyrgyz started a riot at Baren in Akto county, which led to exchanges of fire and a number of deaths. In September 1990 the Xinjiang government produced new regulations tightening controls over religious activities and closing down many mosques and Koranic schools. Yet this was followed by reports of armed insurrections in northwest Xinjiang in spring 1991. Then there was a bomb explosion that wounded a number of people in Urumqi in February 1992.

These events provoked inspection tours by senior PRC leaders, even including Qiao Shi, the Politburo member in charge of national security. Yet in August 1993 Xinjiang Party Secretary Song Hanliang addressed a meeting in Kashi prefecture at which he declared that national separatism still posed a major threat to Xinjiang's stability.[14] And in July 1994 the Chinese authorities ordered a curb on the growing influence of Muslim clerics in the internal affairs of the neighbouring autonomous region of Ningxia, which is worrying because most Muslims there are ethnic Chinese. It is a reminder of the potency of Islamic belief, and the challenge it can pose to the ruling communist party.[15]

Yet security issues are not the only preoccupation of the Chinese authorities. A further set of factors complicates Chinese control of Xinjiang and the northwest. These are economic, and they flow from the reforms which have developed on both sides of the frontier during the 1980s and 1990s. To some extent these factors make Chinese control over Xinjiang more difficult. The opening of frontiers has led to an explosion in cross-border travel as individuals seek new business opportunities. The authorities on both sides of the frontiers are struggling to keep pace with them. On the other hand this expansion of business cuts across ethnic cleavages and therefore may take some force out of ethnic antagonisms.

Economic relations and social consequences

Xinjiang has always been one of the poorer regions of China. For much of the 1980s it suffered further from the consequences of the opening of the national economy to market forces, and the new preferential treatment accorded by the central government to the coastal provinces. In the seventh Five-Year Plan during the second half of the decade, the western provinces of China were explicitly relegated to the role of providers of minerals and raw materials; large-scale modernization projects were to be expected only in the 21st century. It is true that during the 1980s output in Xinjiang grew on average by just over 10 per cent annually, i.e. slightly more than the national average. Nevertheless the share of industry in the total of industrial and agricultural output combined was, at 60 per cent, lower than in other minority regions such as Inner Mongolia and Ningxia. Within the province there was a sense that Xinjiang was being allowed or forced to fall further behind in the race to develop a modern, industrialized economy. Given all its potential for agriculture, animal husbandry, cotton, construction materials and non-ferrous metals, not to mention oil, some felt that it was being held back. Transport infrastructure remained poor, especially in terms of links with the rest of the country.[16] There was a feeling in Xinjiang that it was being exploited by Beijing.

Yet the government of the autonomous region was also dependent upon the central government for subsidies to keep operating. In more recent years up to 50 per cent of its operating budget had to be supported from Beijing. Over the whole period 1950–84 the centre provided 60 per cent of the region's government expenditure.[17] Thus Beijing seemed to be both subsidizing and exploiting Xinjiang.

The growing autonomy that was conceded to all the provinces of China in the 1980s led the authorities in Xinjiang to search for alternatives, and their minds were concentrated by the sharp cuts in investment funds which occurred in 1988 as part of the government's attempts to prevent the economy from overheating, and which hit the western provinces hardest.

In particular the idea of a 'Great Islamic Circle' attracted interest. Initially this meant a turn towards the Middle East.[18] Xinjiang looked for an example to Ningxia, which began its first joint venture with partners from the Gulf states in 1986. Xinjiang too began to try to take advantage of its Muslim identity and trade with partners in the Middle East. The Chinese state attempted to assist this by sending more Chinese students, especially those from the northwestern provinces, to the Middle East to study and learn Arabic (although in absolute terms their numbers remained small).[19] Markets in South Asia also attracted attention.

The collapse of the Soviet Union, however, and the opening of frontiers, made businessmen in Xinjiang look northwards, where they found a particular demand for consumer goods. Markets in Almaty and Tashkent became well stocked with Chinese consumer products. To a limited extent the Central Asian republics, especially Kazakhstan, could reciprocate by exporting oil exploration equipment, tractors and fertilizers.

In the past few years this trade has mushroomed. From an estimated US$88 million in 1988, it reached $1 billion in 1991, and then in 1992 it doubled to $2 billion. In that year the Chinese government attempted to stimulate it still further by granting five cities in Xinjiang equivalent rights to the ten open cities on the east coast for attracting foreign investment, whilst in 1993 it opened ten highways to land ports on the frontiers of republics of the FSU. One Xinjiang official, the Vice-Chairman of the region, predicted that this border trade in 1993 would constitute half of the province's total foreign business.[20] In that case the economic reorientation towards the neighbouring states of Central Asia would reinforce the attraction based upon ethnic ties, although it is not only ethnic minorities who have been doing business across the border.

In the past two years this two-way trade has spread into investments, with Chinese investing in the newly privatized enterprises in Russia, especially Siberia, and also, although to a lesser extent, in Central Asia.[21] In 1992 Xinjiang firms signed a deal to build the largest hotel in Almaty. Clearly this is a trend pointing in the direction of more integrated economies in Central Asia, although it will be a slow process: Kazakh–Chinese joint ventures have not, as yet, been performing as well as expected.

Cross-border tourism and travel have flourished too. In 1992 roughly 130,000 business people and tourists visited Xinjiang from across the border, and in 1993 that figure was expected to rise by 100,000. In fact this is more a cause for concern for the Central Asian authorities, since increasing numbers of Chinese are crossing to do business there. A recent Russian newspaper article estimated that 300–350,000 Chinese were now living in Kazakhstan, especially Almaty: in 1989 none had been listed in the last Soviet census. It was estimated that on average one in ten Chinese crossing the frontier stayed there. More worrying for the Kazakhstan authorities was the involvement of Chinese mafias in the supply and transport of drugs, estimated at US$2 million per year.[22]

Yet although more economic integration is now taking place throughout this region, this is simultaneously drawing in other actors as well, and not just neighbouring ones. It has been argued that Xinjiang's opening to the north could not have been conceived without a similar expansion of its integration into the Chinese economy as a whole.[23] Xinjiang needed the latter so as to supply goods to Central Asia. And, as we shall see, it has also increased the need for foreign investment from outside the region.

Neither China nor Russia, still less the governments of the Central Asian states and Xinjiang, can afford the vast sums which will be needed to exploit all of the resources there. In 1993, for example, China became a net oil importer, and rapid growth has had the effect of making the energy balance even tighter. There is a pressing need for China to develop new sources of oil. Xinjiang is the most likely place.

Yet the central government is being increasingly squeezed for resources, as provinces drag their feet over forwarding the tax revenues to which they had been committed. And the China State Oil Corporation has itself been squeezed, at least until 1993, by a reluctance on the part of the government to allow oil prices to rise to something approaching world market levels, for fear of provoking an upsurge in inflation. Thus the two main domestic sources of potential investments to develop the reserves in Xinjiang, i.e. the government and the National Oil Corporation, are both under strain. It was for these reasons that in 1993, for the first time, Beijing allowed foreign oil companies to participate in onshore oil exploration. Above all this has led to joint exploration in Xinjiang, and a number of oil multinationals are cautiously evaluating the opportunities and risks.

If any of them decide to go ahead with serious exploitation of oilfields there, they will be confronted by the enormous task of shipping the oil to markets. This in turn will require enormous investments in the shape of added railway lines, or an oil pipeline – undertakings for which none of Xinjiang's neighbours will have sufficient resources. So in summer 1993 the Mitsubishi Corporation was commissioned by the Japanese government to begin exploring the possibilities for a gas pipeline linking Xinjiang with the Pacific east coast. Rough estimates have suggested that construction would require trillions of yen, and take nearly a decade. All of this is a reminder that Xinjiang cannot build its own future without significant outside help.

After the strong priority allocated to the coastal regions of China around the middle of the 1980s, there is now a wider recognition among policy-makers in both Beijing and Urumqi of the need for cooperation in developing Xinjiang because it is in the interests of both the autonomous region and the country as a whole.

On the other hand, as was mentioned above, Xinjiang has witnessed an influx of people attracted by the new opportunities for profitable business offered by the economic reforms of the 1980s – one estimate put the figure at over 300,000.[24] Most of these are Han Chinese. The expansion of the oil industry in Xinjiang will inevitably mean a further influx of skilled workers from other parts of China in search of high-paying jobs, again mostly Han Chinese, thus exacerbating the fears among minorities of absorption by the dominant nationality. The influx of foreign tourists, too, largely attracted by the mystique of the Silk Roads, will also make Xinjiang a more cosmopolitan region. Urumqi can now offer a Holiday Inn with CNN satellite television.

What remains problematic is the reaction of local nationalities. One consequence of the increased mobility allowed in China since the 1980s is the greater knowledge that people of one region have about life in other regions of the country. Will people in Xinjiang be grateful for the increased prosperity, or will they be more resentful over the improvements in living standards achieved in Guangdong and elsewhere? And will they attempt to defend their identity, including their religion, more vigorously?

Conclusion

The links developing with the Central Asian states are already gelling into a new economic region which could pull Xinjiang further from Beijing's control. Cross-border ethnic ties, which could underpin economic relations, are re-emerging, and the opportunities for complementary trade are growing. There is a sense that the northern frontier of Xinjiang – and indeed, to a lesser extent, the northern border of the rest of China with the former Soviet Union – has become much more fluid than at any time since 1950s and the heyday of Sino-Soviet cooperation. So Beijing, too, is paying more attention to Central Asia, as changes there accelerate.

Yet it is no longer possible for either Russia or China, or the two of them together, to dominate and control Central Asia as they have attempted to do for centuries. The outside world is now far more active in the region. The prime reason for this is economic, both in terms of needs and of the opportunities which Central Asia and Xinjiang offer. Xinjiang needs not only trade but also investment, so as to be able to open up its rich mineral resources. Here the Central Asian states will be of little assistance, since they themselves are poor and need large amounts of foreign investment if they are to develop their own resources. They will not have anything significant left for aid to Xinjiang. Moreover, they are themselves competitors rather than partners of Xinjiang in terms of mineral endowment, and will want to ensure maximum exploitation of their own resources.

For investment Xinjiang will have to look further afield. The PRC's growing oil shortage will no doubt spur the authorities in Beijing into sympathetic consideration of enhanced rail links, as well as an oil pipeline. On the other hand the growing impoverishment of the central government relative to that of the provinces will act as a brake upon what any province, however significant, can expect.

Like the Central Asian states, the Xinjiang authorities have been courted by both Turkey and Iran – and there have been important visits by the presidents of both these states to Central Asia and to Xinjiang. Yet neither of these countries possesses abundant financial resources. The most important sources of foreign investment would be either oil-rich Muslim states in the Middle East, or Western oil multinationals, or Japan. In any of these cases the source would be relatively distant. Whatever may be the attraction of a regional economic grouping in Central Asia, such as has been mooted by the President of Uzbekistan, it would have to be a region relatively open to the outside world.

In addition Xinjiang's ability to win significant amounts of foreign investment is still, for the moment at least, extremely limited. In 1992 it attracted the second lowest amount of FDI of any provincial-level administration (Tibet was not included in the list). Xinjiang signed contracts for just US$10.5 million, which was more than neighbouring Qinghai, but only a quarter of what Ningxia attracted. It was only 0.01 per cent of all foreign investment contracted to China in that year, and only 0.17 per cent of the total contracted to provincial-level authorities. By contrast Guangdong received 33 per cent.[25]

Moreover, Xinjiang is land-locked. As far as transport is concerned, land-locked countries or regions have little leverage over the neighbours across whose territory trade has to pass – in Xinjiang's case both Russia and China. Xinjiang, like the republics of the FSU in Central Asia, would quickly discover the necessity for preserving reasonably amicable ties with these large neighbours. If China needs Xinjiang's oil, Xinjiang needs China's transport facilities, and probably China's markets, if its oil and other resources are to be sold at competitive prices.

The real threat to harmonious relations with China therefore stems not from economics, but from politics: the dangers of an ethnic upsurge which would spring from resentment over past humiliations, and over the past colonization and misuse of the region's land. This could be reinforced, or sparked off, by grievances over past religious repression. Now most villages in Xinjiang have their own mosque. It is quite possible that minority or religious resentments in some parts of Central Asia might reach Xinjiang, even if they did not originate there. This could result either from economic success or from economic and political failure. On the one hand, growing economic success in Xinjiang might encourage some to press for 'full' independence on the grounds that they could be economically self-sufficient. There is no guarantee that economic success in Xinjiang would lead to a more stable and more quiescent relationship with Beijing. On the other hand, relations between Xinjiang and Beijing might be buffeted as a by-product of other policy changes, causing popular unrest. The introduction of a new fiscal revenue system in 1994 aimed at redirecting more resources to Beijing will, it is feared in Urumqi, increase the region's financial deficit by nearly ten per cent. The Director of the Regional Finance Department called the situation 'very grim'.[26] Or the government in Beijing might feel provoked into intervening in political turbulence on the other side of existing frontiers so as to prevent the spread of destabilization. In turn that could lead to military engagements which might evolve in all sorts of possible directions.

One major change in China's security relationship with Russia has been the emergence over the past fifteen years or so of common security interests in Central Asia. Both China and Russia are concerned at the possible emergence of Islamic regimes in Central Asia, which could provide significant challenges to their respective security situations. Both now have an interest in cooperating to keep the region under control. But will they be able to do so? And even if they are, there must be substantial doubts about the likely effectiveness of their efforts.

7

CONCLUSION

Peter Ferdinand

When the Central Asian states gained their independence in 1991, one of the consequences was a wave of interest around the world. There was great speculation about how they would develop. Some commentators looked forward to a bright future, freed from the Soviet yoke, in which these republics would be able to exploit for their own benefit the enormous natural resources which they possess. The implication for the foreign policies of other countries and for foreign businessmen was that they should become involved in the region as soon as possible for their own good. Others predicted a much more stormy future, seeing the ethnic conflicts of Nagorno-Karabakh, Sumgait and Osh as merely pale shadows of what might happen as nations and clans clashed over land which they regarded as 'theirs'. The implication for outsiders was that they should keep out and, if possible, draw a ring-fence around the region to prevent the conflict from spilling over elsewhere. An almost universal preoccupation was whether the region was going to 'go Islamic fundamentalist', and serve as a catalyst for the same confrontation with the West as had been provoked by the Iranian revolution. This was certainly a fear used by Russian nationalists to make their fellow citizens' skin creep and to win votes.

So far there have been developments in all these directions, but not to the extent of pre-empting others. True, there are tensions and there have been major conflicts and heavy loss of life, above all in Tajikistan. This conflict has in turn been fuelled partly by the smouldering civil war in Afghanistan, and the two continue to spark each other. Yet at least so far, the conflict in Tajikistan has been contained. It has not spread to other parts of Central Asia. Nor have conflicts over territory broken out between other republics.

It is true, too, that achievements have been registered in the economy. Foreign investors have shown some willingness to invest large sums of money on a long-term basis. This is exemplified most strikingly by the Chevron deal in Kazakhstan, but other countries have become involved too, as evidenced by the enormous British Gas investment in Kazakhstan. On the other hand, the region as a whole is far from economic take-off. The sums so far committed from the outside have paled by comparison with the original hopes of people inside the region. And the collapse of the Russian economy has necessarily had an adverse effect upon the economies of Central Asia too.

Islamic fundamentalism has not yet proved the threat that some feared. There have been religious disturbances, even riots, particularly in the Fergana valley. There have been deaths. There is also no doubt that the regimes pay greater attention to Islamic issues and concerns than before. More people from the region make the pilgrimage to Mecca. Where only a few hundred went in 1989, by 1992 the figure had risen to 15,000. President Karimov of Uzbekistan and President Niyazov of Turkmenistan have both been themselves. And the building of mosques has accelerated 150 times in four years. Yet if anything, President Karimov now controls religious life more tightly inside Uzbekistan than he did as leader of the Communist Party.

All of this might suggest that relatively little has changed over the past three years. With the exception (admittedly no small one) of the overthrow of communism as a state doctrine, the changes which have taken place have all been along existing paths rather than breaking new ground.

Yet the overall context of political, social and economic life is now quite different. The situation throughout Central Asia is currently much more fluid than it ever was or could be before the collapse of the Soviet Union. The possibilities for change are greater now and so is the speed at which it might take place. All of the countries dealing with Central Asia which we have surveyed in this book now have a distinct sense of unpredictability about the region, as well as of the need to try to edge changes in the right direction. No avenue of development can be ruled out, whether positive or negative, except probably a return to communism.

Above all, what has changed has been the old ready deference in Central Asia towards outside forces, especially Russia. The states of the region now behave much more as though they were the equals of any partner which courts them. The old sense of being a younger brother overshadowed by an elder brother is disappearing. It is true that the former isolation of the region cannot be overcome immediately. This

Conclusion

partly rested on a transport system controlled through Moscow. Now airlines can fly from the Middle East and Europe direct to Central Asia; it is no longer necessary to fly via Moscow. Transport for heavier goods, however, cannot overcome the legacy of the past so easily. Until more railways, and possibly pipelines, have been built, Central Asia will still be handicapped.

Nevertheless, these enterprises are now being undertaken. By the end of the 1990s great strides will have been made. Then Central Asia will become more fully integrated into the life and economies of its neighbours. Then, too, Central Asia will change from being a region which is just on the receiving end of policies of outsiders. It, or at least some parts of it, will begin to have a more positive impact upon the rest of the world, not just on its neighbours. For some partners both inside and outside Central Asia it will offer significant opportunities. At the very least this will be a transformation that will merit continued observation.

NOTES

Chapter 1: Introduction

1 For a history of the term 'Central Asia' see M. Yapp, 'Tradition and Change in Central Asia', in Shirin Akiner (ed.), *Political and Economic Trends in Central Asia* (London: British Academic Press, 1994), pp. 1–10.

Chapter 2: Post-Soviet Central Asia

1 There is a vast scholarly literature on the early history of Central Asia, much of it devoted to the study of texts and/or religions. The best general survey is given in D. Sinor (ed.), *The Cambridge History of Early Inner Asia* (Cambridge: Cambridge University Press, 1990).

2 For a thorough survey of the development of the Turkic languages and literatures see J. Deny et al. (eds), *Philologiae Turcicae Fundamenta*, 2 vols (Wiesbaden: Franz Steiner Verlag, 1959–65). The educated elite of Transoxiana were bilingual; writers such as Navoi (1441–1501) and Babur (1488–1530) used both languages with equal mastery, a tradition that was maintained into the twentieth century by, for example, Sadriddin Aini (1878–1954), who made a major contribution to the development of Soviet Uzbek as well as Soviet Tajik literature.

3 This is well documented in many sources. A particularly lively account is that given by F.H. Skrine and E.D. Ross, *The Heart of Asia: A History of Russian Turkestan and the Central Asian Khanates from the Earliest Times* (London: Methuen, 1899).

4 The classic Western study of this period is R.A. Pierce, *Russian Central Asia 1867–1917: A Study in Colonial Rule* (Berkeley: University of California Press, 1960). V.V. Bartol'd, *Istoriya kul'turnoy zhizni Turkestana* (Leningrad, AN USSR, 1927), has some very valuable material; so, too, has Eugene Schuyler, *Turkistan: Notes of a Journey in*

111

Russian Turkistan (London: Sampson, Low, Marston, Searle and Rivington, 1876).

5 For a breakdown of the ethnic composition of the republics in 1926, 1959, 1970 and 1979, see the relevant Soviet census reports; a summary of these data is given in Shirin Akiner, *Islamic Peoples of the Soviet Union* (2nd edn) (London: Kegan Paul International, 1986).

6 Frederick C. Barghoorn, *Soviet Russian Nationalism* (Oxford and New York: Oxford University Press, 1956), p. 69.

7 Soviet statements on literacy levels in the Central Asian republics vary slightly, but in general coincide with those given. There is no way of checking them objectively, since the relevant archival material is not available. Most published information relates to Uzbekistan. E. Allworth (*Uzbek Literary Politics*, The Hague, Mouton, 1964, p. 190) is suspicious of the figures for the early 1930s, but accepts the 1939 estimate; W.K. Medlin, W.M. Cave and F. Carpenter (*Education and Development in Central Asia*, Leiden, Brill, 1971, p. 108) are dubious about even this. A detailed survey of the development of the educational network is given by D. Azimova, *Youth and the Cultural Revolution in Soviet Central Asian Republics* (Moscow: Nauka, 1988).

8 For an overview of Soviet language planning policies see M. Kirkwood (ed.), *Language Planning in the Soviet Union* (London: Macmillan, 1989); for a case-study of Uzbekistan, see Shirin Akiner in op. cit. pp. 100–22. An introduction to the creation of Soviet literatures in Central Asia is given in H. Jünger (ed.), *The Literatures of the Soviet Peoples* (New York: Frederick Ungar Publishing Co., 1970).

9 The absurdity of trying to create separate national histories out of a shared cultural heritage, as well as the dangerously proprietorial feelings that such an exercise soon aroused, were well illustrated by the fierce arguments over the ethnic origins of cultural role-models such as Avicenna, al-Farabi and al-Khwarezmi. Ignoring the fact that modern concepts of 'nationality' were entirely inappropriate in a medieval context, it became a point of honour to secure given heroes as part of the exclusive national heritage of each republic.

10 Writers such as Aitmatov speak of the Central Asians as *mankurty*, a reference to a folk tale about a people who lost their memory. See also the poem 'Hatred' by Muhammad Salih (member of *Birlik* and later founder of *Erk*), published in Russian translation as *Nenavist'* (in *Nochnye metafory*, Tashkent, Yash Guardiya, 1989, p. 19), in which, according to the explanation given by Muhammad Salih to the present author, the Central Asians are metaphorically depicted as a sleeping, hate-filled, titanic bird.

11 It was only after the collapse of the Soviet Union, for example, that Uzbek officials first began to discover precisely how much gold was produced annually from the mines on their territory (some 80 tonnes in 1993, making Uzbekistan the eighth largest producer of gold in the world).

12 The term 'sovereignty' in Soviet usage was not synonymous with 'independence'. The full legal implications of the term are not clear, but the chief point at issue appears to have been that certain republican laws would, under certain conditions, take precedence over Soviet laws.

13 There is an interesting parallel in these figures to the results of the French Constitutional Referendum of 1958, which in effect gave the overseas territories the option to declare independence. Only Guinea chose to do so; the remainder were firmly in favour of retaining the links with France, several returning 'yes' votes of 95 per cent and above (see further R. Emerson, *From Empire to Nation*, Cambridge, MA., Harvard University Press, 1967).

14 Prior to 1992 the only foreign consulates in Central Asia were located in Tashkent. They included those of India, Mongolia and Libya. There is now a rapidly increasing number of embassies and trade missions in all five state capitals. High-level delegations to and from the Central Asian republics have become a regular occurrence. Good working relations have been established with nearby countries such as Turkey, Iran, China, India and Pakistan, but also with those further afield, such as South Africa, Australia, Malaysia, Thailand, Japan, South Korea, the US, Canada, most European countries and most Middle Eastern countries (including Israel). See Shirin Akiner (ed.), *Central Asia Newsfile* (hereafter *CAN*) (London: School of Oriental and African Studies), no. 14, December 1993, for a summary of the year's visits.

15 New constitutions have been drafted in all the republics; ministries that were formerly subordinate to central institutions have been upgraded and given new areas of jurisdiction; national financial institutions have been created; new national flags, anthems and emblems have replaced those of the Soviet period. All the republican governments are committed to economic reform, although progress in this direction has so far been sluggish (inevitably, given the lack of a historical background in capitalism and the lack of the necessary skills and services).

16 In Turkmenistan, it was the Ahal-Tekke tribe, Ashkhabad clan, who came to dominate formal and informal power structures; in Kazakhstan, the Great Horde (Ulu Zhus); in Kyrgyzstan, the northern clans. In Uzbekistan there has been some rotation of power between the traditional centres of Fergana, Samarkand and Tashkent; the incumbent president is from the Samarkand group (and is a native speaker of Tajik), but he has succeeded in building up a power base in Tashkent, and at the same time winning over the Fergana group, thus creating a coalition between these traditional rivals. In Tajikistan, the Leninabad/Khojent group came to power in the early Soviet period and remained in control until toppled by the civil war in 1992. As of summer 1994, they seem set to make a come-back, ousting their rivals from Kulyab in the south and Badakhshan in the east.

17 Parliamentary elections were scheduled for the spring of 1994, but by

mid-summer no preparations whatsoever had been undertaken and it seemed unlikely that they could be held with any semblance of order before the late autumn. On 28 December 1993, during the last parliamentary session of the year, the Acting Head of State, Emomali Rakhmonov, announced that he was in favour of a revival of the presidency and would be putting himself forward as a candidate (possibly for election in autumn 1994).

18 It is sometimes supposed that President Akayev has no Communist Party connections; in fact, he, too, held senior office (Head of Ideology in 1986) in the Party. Moreover, he grew up within the same highly politicized environment as the other Central Asian leaders and thus is from a not dissimilar mould.

19 In January 1994, in the run-up to the Kazakh general election of 7 March, Lad was refused registration by the Ministry of Justice on the grounds that it was necessary to have branches in at least 11 of Kazakhstan's 19 provinces. Since Lad's power base is amongst the Russians in the north, they were unable to fulfil this condition. This decision was later reversed and eventually four Lad candidates were elected to the new parliament.

20 However, it should be noted that there is a high turnover of members and of leadership and it is never possible to be sure at any given time what their political stance is likely to be. A good survey of Kyrgyz parties at the end of 1993 is given by Erkin Mamkulov in *Kyrgyzstan Chronicle*, Bishkek, no. 1, 1 December 1993, p. 6.

21 One of the most active Turkmen activists in Moscow is Muhammedmurad Salamatov. He has brought out anti-government publications, e.g. the journal *Dayanch* ('Support'), which commenced publication in 1991; three numbers appeared before it was closed down.

22 Western commentators have frequently written about the supposed activities of Sufi movements in Central Asia, and the importance of such movements in keeping alive the spirit and practice of Islam under Soviet rule. Post-independence, it is clear that no such movements existed (or rather, if they did, they included very few people and were very low-key, interested more in the abstract philosophy of Islam than the belief system as a living force in society). Muslim visitors to Central Asia are constantly astounded by the local population's ignorance of the most basic tenets of the faith.

23 A number of cheap and readily available primers have appeared in shops and street markets recently to popularize the new script, e.g. the Uzbek publication *Lotin yozuvidagi ozbek alifbosini organamiz* ('Let's Learn Uzbek Written in the Latin Script'), A. Ziyadov et al., Tashkent, Mehnat, 1993, which appeared in a print run of 100,000. However, there is much interest in the Arabic script and in some areas (especially the Fergana Valley) shop signs are to be seen in this script. In all the republics, private classes teaching the Arabic script are well attended.

24 Health and education are the sectors that are likely to suffer most. A joint UNICEF–WHO mission which visited the region in early 1992 reported that 'a crisis may be looming'. M. Kaser and S. Mehrotra, *The Central Asian Economies after Independence* (hereafter *Central Asian Economies*), London, Royal Institute of International Affairs, 1992, pp. 51–5.

25 The Head of the State Property Committee, Z. Karibzhanov, announced in July 1993 that a considerable number of the 6,200 privatizations that had been carried out up to that date had involved irregularities and would be cancelled (*CAN*, no. 9, July 1993, p. 7).

26 Personal communication to the author in December 1993 by Erzhan Sag-yndykov, then First Deputy Chairman of the State Committee for Property.

27 See *CAN*, no. 14, December 1993, p. 7; also *Slovo Kyrgyzstana*, 27 November 1993.

28 According to data presented to the Kazakh Cabinet of Ministers on 21 April 1994, there was a contraction of 30% in the GDP for the first quarter of 1994 compared with the same period in 1993. Industrial output was down by 30.9% and capital investment in the state sector by 68.3%. (See *CAN*, vol. 2, no. 5 (19), May 1994, p. 4, for further details; also *CAN*, vol. 1, no. 5, March 1993, p. 5, for figures on economic performance, published by the Kazakh State Committee on Statistics.) The situation is similar in other republics.

29 See, for example, the report in *Petroleum Economist*, February 1994, pp. 19–32.

30 The crude birth-rates per 1,000 in 1987 were: Kazakhstan 25.5; Kyrgyzstan 32.6; Tajikistan 41.8; Turkmenistan 37.2; Uzbekistan 37.0; cf Russian Federation 17.1. The crude death-rates for this period per 1,000 were: Kazakhstan 7.5; Kyrgyzstan 7.3; Tajikistan 6.9; Turkmenistan 7.9; Uzbekistan 6.9; cf Russian Federation 10.5. The rate of natural increase has decreased slightly since 1960, except in Tajikistan, where it has risen. (Source: *Naseleniye SSSR 1987*, Moscow, Finansy i statistika, 1988, pp. 132–42.)

31 In Uzbekistan, for example, levels of population density range from 7.7 per sq. km in Karakalpakstan, which is mostly desert, to 427.4 per sq. km in Andijan Province in the fertile Fergana Valley. (Source: *Narodnoye khozyaistvo Uzbekskoy SSR 1990*, p. 14.)

32 Data for 1989 (Source: *Vestnik statistiki*, Moscow, no. 7, 1991, p. 75).

33 There is an extensive literature on this subject, much of it highly emotional and inclined to uncritical repetition of dubious sources. One of the best recent works is B.Z. Rumer, *Soviet Central Asia: A Tragic Experiment* (Boston: Unwin Hyman, 1989), especially pp. 76–104.

34 For a survey of the main problem areas, see Shirin Akiner, 'Environmental Degradation in Central Asia', in Reiner Weichhardt (ed.), *Economic Developments in Cooperation Partner Countries from a Sectoral Perspective* (Brussels: NATO, 1993), pp. 255–63.

35 The 'Union of People's Unity of Kazakhstan' (generally known by the Russian acronym *SNEK*) is formally led by Kuanish Sultanov, but is very closely linked to the President; it gained 34 seats in the new parliament, almost four times as many as the second largest group, that of the 'People's Congress of Kazakhstan'.

36 There have been a number of intraregional conferences and seminars on the problems of the Aral Sea. Uzbek, Kazakh, Turkmen and Kyrgyz scientists are currently preparing official recommendations for water management in the Aral Sea basin.

37 The local newspapers regularly report instances of drug-related crimes. For a recent report on drug smuggling (including information on prices and routes), see report in *Moskovskiye novosti*, no. 37, 12 September 1993.

38 Kazakhstan expects to be nuclear-free by 1995; however, the question of compensation for the loss of jurisdiction over the strategic missiles has not yet been resolved (*Panorama*, Almaty, no. 18, 7 May 1994, p. 1).

39 See *Central Asian Economies*, pp. 55–6, for an assessment of the effects of this migration.

40 Leaders of the nationalist movements *Erkin Kyrgyzstan, Ata Meken and Asaba* have made numerous public statements on this point. See *CAN*, vol. 2, no. 1 (15), January 1994, p. 5.

Chapter 3: Russian foreign policy and Central Asia

1 A. Benningsen et al., 'The Soviet Islamic establishment as a strategic instrument', in A. Benningsen et al. (eds), *Soviet Strategy and Islam* (New York: St Martin's Press, 1989), p. 22.

2 Alastair McAuley, 'Economic Development and Political Nationalism in Uzbekistan', *Central Asian Survey*, vol. 5, no. 3/4, 1986, p. 182.

3 'Une dictature éclairée au gaz', *Le Monde*, 18 November 1993.

4 For more details, see Mohiaddin Mesbahi, 'Russian foreign policy and security in Central Asia and the Caucasus', *Central Asian Survey*, vol. 12, no. 2, 1993, pp. 181–215.

5 See M.A. Olimov, 'Ob etnopoliticheskoy i konfessional'noy situatsii v Tadzhikistane i veroyatnosti mezhetnicheskikh konfliktov', *Vostok*, 1994 (2), pp. 79–88.

Chapter 4: The Middle East and Central Asia

1 For the purpose of the ensuing discussion, the Middle East is defined as including the areas that two generations ago were known as the Near East and the Middle East. That is, it includes the countries of the Levant and the Arabian Peninsula, together with Egypt, Iran and Turkey, but not the Maghreb.

2 For instance, during a visit to the USSR in November 1991 which com-

prised six of the southern republics, a senior Iranian delegation including the foreign minister, Dr Ali Akbar Velayati, repeatedly stated that Iran was ready 'to expand our political, economic and cultural ties with the Soviet republics *within the framework of our relations with Moscow*' [emphasis added]. See *Kayhan International*, 7 December 1991.

3　For a brief description of this political inheritance see Michael Kaser and Santosh Mehrotra, *The Central Asian Economies After Independence* (London: RIIA, Post-Soviet Business Forum, 1992), pp. 3–4.

4　For a discussion of such tensions in Kazakhstan see Neil Melvin, 'Russia and the ethno-politics of Kazakhstan', in *The World Today*, vol. 49, no. 11, November 1993. See also Adam Dixon, *Kazakhstan: Political Reform and Economic Development* (London: RIIA, Post-Soviet Business Forum, 1994).

5　Edward W. Said, *Orientalism* (Harmondsworth: Penguin, 1985).

6　The waning of the influence of Islam over the past three generations is indicated by the fall in the number of mosques in Central Asia from 20,800 before the Bolshevik revolution to 1,330 official and 2,000 so-called unofficial mosques just prior to the onset of glasnost. See Hélène Carrère d'Encausse, quoted in Daniel Herádstvéit, *Ethnic Conflicts and Refugees in the Former Soviet Union* (Oslo: Norwegian Refugee Council 1993), p. 34.

7　Central Asian leaders were initially wary of Iran. Their tardiness in visiting Tehran contrasted with their rush to visit Ankara, three heads of state travelling to the Turkish capital in December 1991 alone. In June 1992 President Nabiev of Tajikistan visited Iran, and at the end of October 1992 President Nazarbayev of Kazakhstan also made the trip. By this time the initial wariness of Central Asian leaders to be seen to be interacting with Iran had subsided.

8　In summer 1993 Turkish trucks bound for Central Asia experienced problems of access through Iran. See *Turkish Daily News*, 6 August 1993.

9　Michael Brecher, *The Foreign Policy System of Israel* (London: Oxford University Press, 1972), p. 48.

10　For evidence of the Israeli preoccupation with the Muslim confessional background of the new Central Asian states, see the *Jerusalem Post* – for example, 11 January 1992 ('CIS Moslems invite Israelis'); 25 January 1992 ('Jews from Moslem republics get priority').

11　Attributed to Aziz Nesin by Fusun Ozbilgen writing in *Turkish Daily News*, 4 December 1993.

12　The term Wahhabism has been coined to describe the followers of Muhammad ibn Abdul Wahhab, and is used widely in the West. The followers themselves dislike this description and refer to themselves as *muwahhidun* (unitarians). See Patrick Bannerman, *Islam in Perspective* (London: Routledge for the RIIA, 1988), p. 261.

13　*Guardian*, 27 February 1992.

14 *International Herald Tribune*, 24 March 1992.

15 *Christian Science Monitor*, 2 October 1992.

16 Bulent Ecevit during an address at Chatham House, 10 March 1993.

17 See Dr Muhammad Reza Hafiznia writing in *Kayhan International*, 18 June 1992.

18 There are estimated to be some 200,000 Jews in the Republics of Uzbekistan, Azerbaijan, Kazakhstan, Tajikistan and Kyrgyzstan. Of these, 130,000 are Russian-speaking Ashkenazim, 40,000 are Bukharans and 30,000 are from mountain districts. See *Jerusalem Post*, 25 January 1992. With 23,000 Jews estimated to be still living in Azerbaijan (see *Jerusalem Post*, 11 January 1992), the total number of Jews in Central Asia would be in the region of 175,000.

19 For instance, a joint US–Israeli company was to be established to raise funds for agricultural projects in Central Asia. See statement by Amaran Olmert in *Ma'ariv*, reprinted in *Turkish Daily News*, 24 November 1993.

20 See press conference with CIS assistant coordinator Richard Armitage, 29 July 1992, reprinted in undated *European Wireless File*.

21 *The Financial Times*, 6 May 1992.

22 *The Financial Times*, 26 November 1992.

23 *The Financial Times*, 28 January 1993.

24 Ibid.

25 Interview with Shirin Akiner, 2 December 1992.

26 See *The Financial Times*, 15 April 1992 in which Michael Field emphasizes the limited potential of Iranian influence in Central Asia.

27 *The Financial Times*, 14 May 1992.

28 *International Herald Tribune*, 12 May 1992.

29 *Christian Science Monitor*, 14 August 1992.

30 *Kayhan International*, 23 July 1992.

31 During a visit President Rafsanjani paid to Almaty in October 1993, a letter of understanding was signed in which, among other things, the two sides agreed to connect their railways to the Asian rail network, to expand marine transportation and to establish flight links between the two capitals. See *Kayhan International*, 28 October 1993.

32 *The Financial Times*, 23 June 1992.

33 *The Financial Times*, 4 December 1992.

34 For instance, in Azerbaijan the Karabakh war and its consequences have deterred a major economic engagement by Turkish firms.

35 Laura Le Cornu, 'Turkmenistan–Turkish Relations', unpublished paper commissioned by the author based on a study visit to Ashkhabad.

Chapter 5: Central Asia's relations with Afghanistan and South Asia

1 Interviews with Moscow Central TV of 8 and 10 October 1991.
2 See further Henry S. Bradsher, *Afghanistan and the Soviet Union* (Durham, NC: Duke UP, 1985); Anthony Hyman, *Afghanistan Under Soviet Domination* (London: Macmillan, 1992); R. Nyrop and D. Seekins (eds), *Afghanistan. A Country Study* (Washington, DC: The American University, 1986).
3 Alexander Umnov, 'The Afghan Crisis and Tajikistan', in *Russia and the Moslem World Bulletin* (Moscow), no. 2, 1992.
4 See Graham E. Fuller, *The 'Centre of the Universe': the Geopolitics of Iran* (Boulder, CO: Westview, 1991), p. 232.
5 Quoted from an interview with Jean Radvanyi, in *Le Cinéma d'Asie centrale soviétique* (Paris: Editions du Centre Pompidou, 1991).
6 See further Craig Baxter, 'Pakistan become prominent in the international arena', Chapter 6 in S.H. Burki and C. Baxter (eds), *Pakistan Under the Military* (Boulder, CO: Westview, 1991), and A. Hyman, *Pakistan: Towards a Modern Muslim State?* (London: Research Institute for the Study of Conflict and Terrorism, 1990).
7 Quoted from Robert Wirsing, *Pakistan's Security under Zia, 1978–88* (New York: St Martin's Press, 1991), p. 7.
8 On Pakistani ambitions, see further Dietrich Reetz's article on Pakistan in the *Journal of South Asian and Middle Eastern Studies*, Villanova, PA, fall issue 1993.
9 BBC *Summary of World Broadcasts*, SWB, 8 January 1993.
10 *The Muslim* (Islamabad), 27 November 1992.
11 Report in *The Pakistan Times*, 11 October 1992.
12 Peter Lyon, 'South Asia and the Geostrategics of the 1990s', in *Contemporary South Asia*, Oxford, 1992, vol. 1.

Chapter 6: The new Central Asia and China

For a slightly different perspective on relations between Central Asia and China, see Peter Ferdinand, 'Xinjiang: Relations with China and Abroad', in David S.G. Goodman and Gerald Segal (eds), *China Deconstructs: Politics, Trade and Regionalism* (London: Routledge, forthcoming 1995).

1 See, for example, Dru Gladney, 'The Ethnogenesis of the Uighur', *Central Asian Survey*, vol. 9, no. 1, 1990, pp. 1–28.
2 Owen Lattimore, *Inner Asian Frontiers of China* (Boston: Beacon Press, 1940), p. 171.
3 Allen S. Whiting and General Sheng Shih-ts'ai, *Sinkiang: Pawn or Pivot?* (East Lansing: Michigan State UP, 1958), p. 14.
4 United States Consulate General, Hong Kong, *Survey of the China Mainland Press*, no. 212, 1951, p. 13; no. 220, 1951, p. 14; cited in June Teufel

Dreyer, 'The PLA and Regionalism: Xinjiang Province' (forthcoming).

5 *Zhongguo sheng qing* (Beijing, 1986), p. 964.

6 *Far Eastern Economic Review*, 25 August 1988, pp. 28–9.

7 Figures taken from Thomas Hoppe, 'Die chinesische Position in Ost-Turkestan/Xinjiang', *CHINA aktuell*, June 1992, p. 360.

8 Eden Naby, 'Uighur Elites in Xinjiang', *Central Asian Survey*, vol. 5, nos 3/4, 1986, p. 249.

9 Yuan Ming, 'Missed Historic Opportunity Recalled', *Minzhu Zhongguo*, no. 8, February 1992, pp. 17–18 (translated in JPRC-CAR–92–039).

10 Naby, op. cit, p. 243.

11 Oskar Weggel, 'Islamischer Fundamentalismus, pantürkischer Integrationismus oder chinesischer Reformismus?', *CHINA aktuell*, April 1994, p. 390.

12 *International Herald Tribune*, 20 April 1994.

13 *CHINA aktuell*, April 1994, p. 392.

14 'Xinjiang Secretary Addresses Prefectural Meeting', FBIS-CHI–93–162, 24 August 1993, p. 63.

15 *The Times*, 18 July 1994, p. 13.

16 Li Fang, 'Xinjiang jingji he shehui fazhandi jige wenti', *Minzu Yanjiu*, 1993(2), pp. 17–18.

17 Ibid., p. 17; *Zhongguo sheng qing*, p. 960.

18 Gayle Christofferson, 'Xinjiang and the Great Islamic Circle: the Impact of Transnational Forces on Chinese Regional Economic Planning', *China Quarterly*, 133 (March 1993), p. 133.

19 Dru Gladney, 'Transnational Islam and Uighur National Identity: Salman Rushdie, Sino-Muslim Missile Deals, and the Trans-Eurasian Railway', *Central Asian Survey*, vol. 11, no. 3, 1992, pp. 11–13.

20 *Beijing Review*, 1–7 February 1993, p. 27.

21 E. Grebenshchikov, 'Vaucher kak predmet eksporta', *Aziya i Afrika Segodniya*, 1993(5), pp. 49–50.

22 'China-Towny v Kazakhstanskikh gorodakh', *Nezavisimaia gazeta*, 7 October 1993.

23 Christofferson, op. cit.

24 BBC *Summary of World Broadcasts*, FE/2008/G11, 28 May 1994.

25 *JETRO Chinese Newsletter*, no. 105, July–August 1993, p. 22.

26 *SWB* FEW/0333 W52/4.